T012409G

MACBETH

THE BOOK, CD-ROM, AND WEBSITE THAT WORK TOGETHER

PRINCETON · LONDON

www.two-canpublishing.com

Two-Can Publishing LLC
234 Nassau Street, Princeton, NJ 08542

Created by
Picthall & Gunzi Ltd
21A Widmore Road, Bromley, Kent BR1 1RW, UK

Consultant: Jane Buckland

BOOK
Story: Barnaby Harward
Editors: Barnaby Harward, Lauren Robertson,
Jill Somerscales, Deborah Murrell, Karen Dolan
Design & Production: Paul Calver
Illustrator: Ray Bryant

CD-ROM
Writers: Barnaby Harward, Deborah Murrell
Editors: Lauren Robertson, Jill Somerscales, Karen Dolan
Illustrator: Ray Bryant
Voices: Mike Evans, Sarah Jones,
Judy Liebert, Christopher Williams

Art Director: Chez Picthall
Editorial Director: Christiane Gunzi

CD-ROM created by
Q&D Multimedia
Producer: Rachel Hall
Programmer: Chris Henson
Sound: Peter Hall
Graphics: Tony Hall

© Two-Can Publishing 2001

"Two-Can," "Interfact," and "Interfact Shakespeare" are trademarks of Two-Can Publishing
Two-Can Publishing is a division of Zenith Entertainment Ltd,
43–45 Dorset Street, London W1U 7NA, UK

For more information on Two-Can books and multimedia, call 1-609-921-6700,
fax 1-609-921-3349, or visit our website at http://www.two-canpublishing.com

ISBN 1-58728-382-4

2 4 6 8 10 9 7 5 3 1

Printed in Hong Kong by Wing King Tong, Hong Kong
Color reproduction by Next Century Ltd, Hong Kong

INTERFACT SHAKESPEARE ™

THE BOOK, CD-ROM, AND WEBSITE THAT WORK TOGETHER

INTERFACT SHAKESPEARE will have you mesmerized in minutes—*and that's a fact!*

◆ The INTERFACT CD-ROM is packed with games and activities that are challenging, fun, and full of fascinating facts.

◆ Open the book and read *Macbeth*. You can also find out the historical background of the play and read our version of the story, written in modern English.

◆ Visit the INTERFACT SHAKESPEARE WEBSITE and surf links to everything the student of Shakespeare might need to know, including a Homework Helper.

◆ To get the most out of INTERFACT SHAKESPEARE, use the book, CD-ROM, and website together. And look out for DISK LINKS and BOOKMARKS. For more information, turn to page 110.

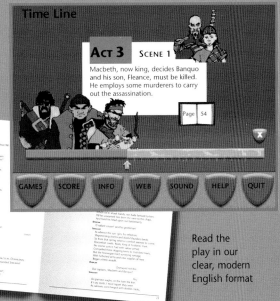

Use the TIME LINE to discover how the plot unfolds

Time Line

ACT 3 SCENE 1
Macbeth, now king, decides Banquo and his son, Fleance, must be killed. He employs some murderers to carry out the assassination.

Page 54

GAMES   SCORE   INFO   WEB   SOUND   HELP   QUIT

Read the play in our clear, modern English format

BOOKMARK

| ACT 3 | PAGE |
| SCENE 1 | 56 |

DISK LINK
Guess what Shakespeare's more difficult words and phrases mean in the GLOSSARY GAME.

LOAD UP!
Go to page 107 to find out how to load your CD-ROM and click into action.

WHAT'S ON THE CD-ROM?

HELP SCREEN

Do you need some assistance? Access the Help Screen and learn how to use the CD-ROM in no time at all.

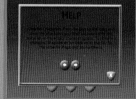

Become familiar with the controls and find out how to use:
◆ the games;
◆ the information screens;
◆ the scoring screen.

GLOSSARY GAME

Speak'st thou Shakespearean? Play this game and thou shalt be a merry prattler indeed!

Discover the meaning of many of Shakespeare's most unusual and wonderful words and phrases, and learn some of the English language's most exciting vocabulary.

WALK-THROUGH MACBETH

How well do you know the plot? Test your knowledge and learn some more.

Put on your thinking cap and answer a series of multiple-choice questions on *Macbeth*. The game is full of information which will give you an in-depth understanding of the play.

OFF WITH HIS HEAD

Put your knowledge to the test and help Macduff save Scotland from Macbeth's evil ways.

Macbeth must die if Scotland is to be free. Macduff can only kill him when you have answered enough questions correctly. Are you up to the challenge?

MAKE A SCENE

Can you remember the characters, props, and sound effects in the most important scenes of the play?

Test your memory of *Macbeth* in our drag-and-drop game and see if you know who and what you would need if you were directing the key parts of the play.

TIME LINE

Remind yourself of the storyline with our quick-reference time line.

***Macbeth* is a long play and sometimes it can be difficult to follow the order of the action. Use the Time Line to refresh your memory of the play's most significant events.**

WHO SAID WHAT?

Shakespeare's plays are full of famous quotations, but do you know which characters say which ones?

Decide for yourself who you think said which quotation and they will tell you if you're right or wrong. But watch out! Some of the characters will really tell you if you make a mistake.

MEET THE CHARACTERS

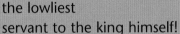
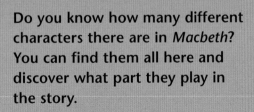

This introduces all the different characters in the play, from the lowliest servant to the king himself!

Do you know how many different characters there are in *Macbeth*? You can find them all here and discover what part they play in the story.

WHAT'S IN THE BOOK?

What's on the Website?

From the Interfact Shakespeare website you can link to all the best Shakespeare sites on the web. If you're a student or a teacher, or just trying to find out more about the Bard's work, start your research here.

Sites on Shakespeare
From all the links to sites on Shakespeare himself, you can check out Shakespeare titles on the Worldbook site or take a virtual tour of Stratford-upon-Avon with Shakespeare's Birth Place Trust.

Sites on the Globe Theatre
The many sites listed on the Globe Theatre include a link to a map of London in 1600, created by the *Encyclopedia Britannica*, and a performance in a virtual theater when you visit Shakey's Place.

Sites for Students
Shakespeare is made easy here. From the links listed, you can enter the Shakespeare Classroom, the best site on the net for Shakespeare students, or try the Shakespeare Homework Helper and finish that essay.

Sites for Teachers
From the Interfact Shakespeare website teachers can link to, among other things, the complete works of Shakespeare or a site offering advice on the correct pronunciation of Shakespearean English.

PREFACE

by Harold Bloom,
Sterling Professor of the Humanities,
Yale University

It is no surprise that William Shakespeare more than anticipated the phenomenon of multimedia: he invented it. His plays deliberately refuse to stay within the restricted space of the Globe Theatre, since he was at once the most practical and the most imaginative of all dramatists. Motion pictures, television, CD-ROMs, gameplaying, voiceovers, light and sound spectaculars, even virtual reality are all prophesied in the full range of his total production. At his most visionary, in *Macbeth*, *A Midsummer Night's Dream*, *Antony and Cleopatra*, and *The Tempest*, Shakespeare exhausts even our current multimedia resources. He remains an ongoing challenge to fresh developments in the technology of presentation.

Because Shakespeare writes both for the inner and the outer ear, and for the inward and the outward eye, his art makes us highly conscious of how total a response is called for on our part. Bottom, describing what he calls his "dream" of transformation in *A Midsummer Night's Dream*, tells us that:

> "The eye of man hath not heard, the ear of man
> hath not seen, man's hand is not able to taste,
> his tongue to conceive, nor his heart to report
> what my dream was."
>
> Act 4 Scene 1

Bottom has had "a most rare vision," that calls out for multimedia and beyond. We need an eye that can hear, an ear that can see, a hand able to taste, a tongue that can think, and a heart that can speak if we are to apprehend Shakespeare. Chorus, speaking the prologue to *King Henry V*, urges us, as audience, to aid the actors, "Piece out our imperfections with your thoughts." And so we must, so extraordinary and vivid are Shakespeare's imaginings.

Macbeth goes into trance-like states, in which he has second sight, "and nothing is/But what is not." We need to hear him, but also to read him, and then we need to see, through his eyes, what cannot be clutched, an imaginary dagger that becomes bloodied, even as he (and we) gaze upon it.

Shakespeare provides an education of all the senses, as well as of the mind and the heart. When, in Act 5 of *Twelfth Night*, Sebastian and the disguised Viola are revealed as identical twins, except for gender, the Duke Orsino cries out:

> "One face, one voice, one habit, and two persons,
> A natural perspective, that is and is not!"
> Act 5 Scene 1

Orsino means that he sees an optical illusion engendered by nature, rather than one produced by a perspective glass, an Elizabethan multimedia toy. Dr. Samuel Johnson, greatest of English critics, commented upon "a natural perspective" that nature so puts on "a show, where shadows seem realities, where that which 'is not' appears like that which 'is.'" I think that Johnson shrewdly realizes that *Twelfth Night* is a compound toy, a distorting mirror whirling in circles, like a top. This confirms the clown Feste's remark in the play, when he says of Malvolio's predicament, "and thus the whirligig of time brings on his revenges." Shakespeare again anticipates the puzzles, games, and discoveries that children and adults bring to him, and find in him ever more richly than they could have expected.

Mercutio, the bawdy wit of *Romeo and Juliet*, sums up the multimedia prophecy of Shakespeare in his wonderful speech about Queen Mab (Act 1 Scene 4). When Mercutio says of this mischievous fairy that, "Her chariot is an empty hazelnut, made by the joiner squirrel," Shakespeare intends to startle us into a new way of seeing. That may be why Shakespeare is most essential to all of us. He showed us first that all our supposed facts are really interfaces.

Harold Bloom

HISTORICAL BACKGROUND

by Jane Buckland,
Educational Consultant

Shakespeare's career as an actor and playwright began when he moved to London from Stratford-upon-Avon around 1590. While his family stayed in Stratford, William Shakespeare became a wealthy and popular writer and part owner of London's Globe Theatre.

Permanent theaters were new at the time, and Shakespeare's plays were among the first to be performed in them. Acting companies were made up entirely of male actors, with boys playing the female roles. Shakespeare's plays were popular with ordinary people who came to see his performances at The Globe, The Curtain, and The Theatre. They were also performed to England's aristocracy, and Shakespeare was a favorite of both Queen Elizabeth I and King James I. James I liked Shakespeare's acting company so much that he allowed them the honor of calling themselves The King's Men.

Macbeth was written sometime around 1606, three years after King James I succeeded Elizabeth I as sovereign of England. James was already King of Scotland when he inherited the English throne, so he is officially titled James VI and I. To win the king's favor, Shakespeare wrote a play about James' Scottish ancestors. Macbeth, King Duncan, Malcolm, Donalbain, and Banquo were real people who lived in eleventh-century Scotland.

Although it is true that the real Macbeth killed King Duncan, Shakespeare's play is not historically accurate. Banquo, James' ancestor, is shown to be an honorable man, but in the true story he may have actually helped Macbeth kill King Duncan!

There are a number of flattering references to King James in the play, including a mention of all the English kings' special powers of healing, an ability which James proudly believed he had inherited. Another reference is an allusion to James' descendents. In the apparition of a line of kings in the witches' cavern, the last king, representing James, holds up a mirror, showing that the royal line goes on forever.

We consider any murder terrible, and so would the people of Shakespeare's time, but the murder of a king, or "regicide," would have been thought of as particularly awful. Just before Shakespeare wrote *Macbeth*, there had been an attempt to murder King James by Guy Fawkes and the other members of the famous Gunpowder Plot. The plot was discovered and the perpetrators were executed. Shakespeare's reminder in *Macbeth* that crime doesn't pay, especially when it's regicide, would have been timely.

Most people believed that whatever happened to the king affected the whole country and everyone in it. Peace and harmony would only exist if everybody kept to their place in society, from the king down to the poorest beggar, and only God was above the king. On the night that Macbeth kills Duncan in the play, a character describes an owl killing a falcon, and horses going mad and eating each other. These events are meant to be a sign that the unnatural act of killing a king would bring about chaos.

Shakespeare's use of witches in *Macbeth* also stems from the interests of the king. James believed strongly in witchcraft and had written a book on the subject. He introduced a law to punish with execution anyone found guilty of practicing witchcraft, and he even believed that witches had once tried to kill him by causing a storm at sea, just like the witches do in the play.

It was not just King James who was fascinated by witchcraft. At this time, the witchcraze was rampaging across Europe and all levels of society had a strong belief in the danger of evil. All children born in England were baptized into the Church of England and attendance at church was mandatory. For Shakespeare's audience, witchcraft and the power of witches were very real and very frightening. Macbeth's story, as he is led further and further into wickedness by the witches, would have shocked and excited any seventeenth-century audience.

Today *Macbeth* can still be shocking. To modern audiences, however, it is not the supernatural side of the story that is frightening, but the moral one. The tale of a man whose evil deeds lead him to be so consumed by guilt that his life becomes a living hell applies as much today as it did 400 years ago.

THE STORY OF
MACBETH
A tale of murder and treachery

INTRODUCTION

Shakespeare's language is four centuries old. Many of the words he used have changed in meaning or disappeared from common use and some phrases can be difficult to understand for modern readers. It can be helpful to know the basic story line of the play before you read the original text or even before you see a theater or film production.

The aim of this story is just that—to help you understand what you are reading when you approach the play text. In this version of the story the action closely follows the play. Act and scene references are included so that you can look things up in the play text while reading the story and vice versa. However, some artistic license has been taken in much the same way that actors and directors bring their own ideas to a performance of a Shakespearean play. Not every scene from the play is included as some of them are not essential to understanding the plot.

Any quotations in the story are taken directly from the play. Many of these are the more famous lines and are explained in the text if their meaning is not obvious.

Reading the story will help you to play the games on the CD-ROM, but if you want to know all the answers you will need to look at the play itself. Have fun. Entertainment is what Shakespeare is all about!

THE STORY

Act 1 Scene 3

In the days when King Duncan ruled Scotland, there lived a brave general named Macbeth. He was a cousin of the king and was highly respected by all the nobility of Scotland.

One evening when Macbeth and his good friend Banquo were returning from a victorious battle, they met three witches on a barren and empty heath.

"All hail, Macbeth, hail to thee, Thane of Glamis! All hail, Macbeth, hail to thee, Thane of Cawdor! All hail, Macbeth, that shalt be king hereafter!" cried the witches in greeting.

It was true that Macbeth was Thane of Glamis, but he was not Thane of Cawdor, and most certainly not king.

Believing the witches were somehow predicting Macbeth's future, Banquo asked what they could tell him. They answered that, although Banquo would never be king, his sons would become kings. Then the witches disappeared and left the two men feeling very confused.

Just then some messengers rode up and told Macbeth that King Duncan had rewarded him for his recent victory with a new title—Thane of Cawdor.

"What!" said Banquo, "can the devil speak true?"

Macbeth was equally amazed and, being a highly ambitious man, wondered if the prophecy that he would become king would also soon come true. Of course that would be impossible while King Duncan lived. But if Duncan were dead…

Act 1 Scene 5   Several days later, King Duncan decided to stay the night at Macbeth's castle. Macbeth had told his wife about the witches' prophecy and Lady Macbeth, who was as ambitious as her husband and prepared to carry out any evil to get what she wanted, decided that they should take the opportunity to murder Duncan that night as he slept.

Act 1 Scene 7   Macbeth was not at all certain of his wife's plan, as at heart he was loyal to his king. He voiced his doubts to Lady Macbeth saying he would only do what came naturally to him as a human being. Murdering a man he respected was unnatural and therefore beyond his capabilities.

"I dare do all that may become a man," he said. "Who dares do more is none."

But she would hear none of it. She was a beautiful and clever woman and she knew how to get her husband to do as she pleased. Explaining how she planned to get Duncan's servants drunk before they went to sleep, she soon persuaded Macbeth to carry out the evil deed.

Act 2 Scene 1   The night was as black as pitch and the wind howled around the battlements. As Macbeth made his way through the castle's dark corridors towards Duncan's chamber, a strange vision of a dagger appeared in front of him.

"Is this a dagger which I see before me, the handle toward my hand?" he asked himself. "Come, let me clutch thee."

But there was nothing there — just a spectral image shimmering in the darkness.

At that moment, a bell rang and the dagger disappeared. Macbeth shook his head to clear his thoughts.

"The bell invites me," he said. "Hear it not, Duncan, for it is a knell that summons thee to heaven or to hell."

Act 2 Scene 2

When Macbeth returned to his chamber, Lady Macbeth was awake and waiting for him. His hands were covered in blood and he still held the daggers with which he had murdered his king. He was shaking with fear and disgust at what he had done.

"Methought I heard a voice cry, 'Sleep no more! Macbeth does murder sleep,'" he whispered. "'Glamis hath murdered sleep, and therefore Cawdor shall sleep no more! Macbeth shall sleep no more!'"

Lady Macbeth told him to go back and leave the daggers in Duncan's room but he refused to return to the grizzly scene. Instead she took them back herself and smeared blood on the drunken servants who slept there to make it look as if they were guilty of the murder.

Act 2 Scene 3

As the sky gradually grew light, Macduff, Thane of Fife, and a nobleman named Lennox, arrived at the castle. Macduff went to wake the king and, discovering the terrible scene, rushed back to the courtyard with the news. Macbeth was there talking with Lennox.

"O horror! horror! horror!" cried Macduff. "Tongue nor heart cannot conceive nor name thee!"

Macbeth and Lennox raced up to Duncan's chamber and finding the sleepy servants still covered with blood—and apparently guilty of the murder—Macbeth killed them both.

The whole castle was in commotion. Duncan's two sons, Malcolm and Donalbain, were afraid that they, too, were in danger and decided to leave Macbeth's castle as soon as possible. Malcolm, the elder, chose to go to England and Donalbain to Ireland.

Act 2 Scene 4

Malcolm and Donalbain's hurried escape turned out to be very lucky for Macbeth. Rumors began to spread that they were guilty of their father's murder and had paid Duncan's servants to be their assassins. Without any opposition, Macbeth was crowned the new king and moved to the royal palace.

Act 3 Scene 1

So Macbeth had it all—exactly according to the witches' prophecy. But he still felt very ill at ease, particularly with Banquo, who suspected that he had not played by the rules.

"Thou hast it now," said Banquo, "king, Cawdor, Glamis, all, as the weird women promised, and, I fear, thou playedst most foully for't."

Banquo also remembered the second part of the witches' prophecy—that *his* sons and not Macbeth's would be future kings of Scotland.

"Yet it was said," Banquo continued, "it should not stand in thy posterity, but that myself should be the root and father of many kings."

Frightened that his friend knew too much, Macbeth began to plot Banquo's murder. In order to prevent the witches' prophecy from coming true, Macbeth had to see that Banquo's son, Fleance, was also killed. He invited Banquo and Fleance to a feast and hired three murderers who would kill the two men as they arrived at the palace.

Act 3 Scene 3 — Banquo and Fleance were just approaching the palace walls when the murderers leaped upon them.

"O, treachery!" cried Banquo. "Fly, good Fleance, fly, fly, fly!" As the three murderers brutally hacked the defenseless Banquo to a bloody pulp, Fleance made his escape. The murderers raced after him but they could not catch him and soon gave up the chase. They returned to Macbeth to report what they had done.

Act 3 Scene 4 — Macbeth heard the news as the feast was just about to begin. Once more he sank into a fit of anxiety. His position on the throne, and that of his heirs, would never be secure if Banquo's sons were destined to be kings.

He asked all the guests to be seated and then looked for an empty place for himself. There was none. Instead, in the chair that Macbeth was supposed to occupy sat a horrific sight—the bloody and beaten ghost of Banquo. White with fear and hardly able to stand, Macbeth shouted at the ghost, "Thou canst not say I did it. Never shake thy gory locks at me."

The guests, to whom the ghost was invisible, were shocked at Macbeth's outburst. What had gotten into the king? Why was he acting so strangely? Lady Macbeth tried to calm them and told her husband to pull himself together but Macbeth could not be controlled. Worried that her husband might give away their guilt about the murders, Lady Macbeth hurriedly asked the guests to leave.

They left and rumors as to the meaning of what they had just witnessed began spreading like wildfire.

In the empty banquet hall, Macbeth slumped into a chair. Head in his hands, he compared his situation to crossing a river of blood, where returning would be as difficult as carrying on: "I am in blood stepped in so far that, should I wade no more, returning were as tedious as go o'er."

Taking her husband by the arm, Lady Macbeth led him along the cold passageways to their bed chamber.

Act 4 Scene 1

Macbeth hardly slept. Every night since the murder his dreams had been filled with images of murder and death and every little noise made him jump out of his skin. He simply could not carry on this way and decided he must find the witches and discover from them what the future held.

In a dingy cavern the witches waited for Macbeth—they knew that he would come.

"Double, double toil and trouble; fire burn and cauldron bubble," they sang as they hurled the foul ingredients of their infernal craft into a huge cooking pot.

"How now, you secret, black, and midnight hags!" said Macbeth as he came in, and he demanded that they reveal to him his future.

They showed him three apparitions, which appeared in front of Macbeth, shining brightly in the gloom.

The first, a head wearing a helmet, told Macbeth to beware of Macduff. The second, a baby, all covered in blood and gore, said that Macbeth need fear no man that was born of a woman. The third—a child holding a tree—stated that Macbeth had no need to worry until Birnam Wood moved to his castle at Dunsinane.

Macbeth had one more question for the witches—what would become of Banquo's sons? In answer he saw a line of kings with Banquo's ghost following them. Then suddenly the apparition and the witches vanished.

Except for the last, these prophecies gave Macbeth hope. What did he have to fear if no man born from a woman could hurt him? Was it likely that a forest would uproot itself and move across the countryside? Macduff should be easy to dispose of, except that he had gone to England to join Prince Malcolm. Just to be safe, though, Macbeth sent some assassins to take care of Macduff's wife and children.

Act 4 Scene 2

Lady Macduff was sitting with her young son when the murderers burst in. When one of them accused Macduff of being a traitor, the boy cried: "Thou liest, thou shag-haired villain!"

Furious that he should be insulted by a child, the assassin screamed, "What, you egg! Young fry of treachery!" and thrust his sword deep into the boy's stomach.

As she tried to escape, another murderer grabbed Lady Macduff and cold-bloodedly slit her throat. With their taste for blood whetted, the murderers went on a killing spree throughout Macduff's castle.

After such wholesale slaughter, not one of Macduff's children, nor even a single servant, was left alive.

Act 4 Scene 3 Macduff was in the English king's palace speaking with Malcolm when a messenger arrived from Scotland.

"Stands Scotland where it did?" asked Macduff.

They discussed Macbeth's continuing tyranny and the sorry state of their homeland, then the messenger broke the news about Macduff's family.

"What, all my pretty chickens and their dam at one fell swoop?" asked the distraught man.

There was no denying it—all his children and their mother were dead. Macduff vowed to take revenge on Macbeth and immediately he and Malcolm began to make preparations for an invasion of Scotland.

Act 5 Scene 1 For some days, Lady Macbeth's gentlewoman, or personal servant, had been worried about her lady's health. Several times she had been woken in the night by Lady Macbeth sleepwalking and mumbling strange and senseless things to herself as she walked.

She arranged for a doctor to stay over at the castle and together they sat up waiting for Lady Macbeth to appear. As they sat speaking in soft voices in the shadows, Lady Macbeth came into the room. The gentlewoman and the doctor were transfixed by what they saw and heard.

"Out, damned spot! out, I say!" cried Lady Macbeth and she rubbed her hands together as if she were washing them. "Yet who would have thought the old man to have had so much blood in him."

The doctor could hardly believe his ears. Was that not an admission of guilt for Duncan's murder? And there was more.

"The Thane of Fife had a wife. Where is she now?" continued the sleeping woman. Then, groaning as if she were on her death bed, "Here's the smell of the blood still. All the perfumes of Arabia will not sweeten this little hand. Oh, oh, oh!"

When Lady Macbeth finally returned to bed, the doctor told the gentlewoman that her illness was more mental than physical and there was nothing he could do.

"Foul whisperings are abroad," he added. "Unnatural deeds do breed unnatural troubles."

Act 5 Scene 4 After marching for several days, an army, led by Malcolm and Macduff, arrived at Birnam Wood. Malcolm ordered the soldiers each to cut down a branch of a tree with which they would camouflage themselves as they advanced towards Macbeth's headquarters at Dunsinane Castle.

Act 5 Scene 5 In the castle, Macbeth prepared for war. His spies had kept him informed of the invading army's movements and he had fortified Dunsinane and made it ready to hold off a siege.

As he was putting on his armor, he heard a woman screaming in a nearby chamber.

"Wherefore was that cry?" he asked a servant who had just entered the room.

"The queen, my lord, is dead."

Although Macbeth had become almost impervious to pain and death, this news shook him to the core. What point was there to life, he thought, this daily toil toward an inevitable death? What idiots men were to think that life has meaning when everything they do is forgotten as soon as they are dead.

"Tomorrow, and tomorrow, and tomorrow," he said out loud, "creeps in this petty pace from day to day to the last syllable of recorded time, and all our yesterdays have lighted fools the way to dusty death. Out, out, brief candle! Life's but a walking shadow, a poor player that struts and frets his hour upon the stage and then is heard no more. It is a tale told by an idiot, full of sound and fury, signifying nothing."

A knock at the door brought Macbeth out of this reverie. A messenger entered and gave him some terrifying news—Birnam Wood was moving! It was coming this way, towards Dunsinane.

"Liar and slave!" roared Macbeth. "If thou speak'st false, upon the next tree shalt thou hang alive."

A glance out of the window proved that the man had spoken the truth and, with little hope that he stood any chance of victory, Macbeth led his small army of remaining supporters to meet his fate.

Act 5 Scene 7 Having thrown off their camouflage, Malcolm's army was ready for battle. The two forces met and the fighting raged around Dunsinane's massive walls.

Macbeth fought wildly, his sword slashing and flailing at any soldier who dared approach. What did he have to live for? And anyway, the king feared no man, or at least no man of woman born.

Act 5 Scene 8 Then he heard a call behind him: "Turn, hellhound, turn!" bellowed Macduff over the terrible din of battle.

Their swords clashed and they fought madly, the two most powerful men on the field.

In between blows, Macbeth told Macduff of the witches' prophecy and the charmed life he lived. Macduff could not kill him, nor could anyone else, he said.

"Despair thy charm!" smiled Macduff grimly. "And let the angel whom thou still hast served tell thee, Macduff was from his mother's womb untimely ripped."

Macbeth almost dropped his sword at these words. Could this be true? Macduff had not had a natural birth, but instead had been delivered by Cesarean section.

What chance had Macbeth now? His fate was sealed. His small army was losing the battle and he would never let himself be humiliated and beg Malcolm for mercy. He must fight, and fight to the death.

"Lay on, Macduff," he called, "and damned be him that first cries, 'Hold, enough!'"

Act 5 Scene 9

The battle was over and Malcolm's forces had won the day. Inside the castle the prince gathered his generals about him to celebrate their victory. But no one had seen Macduff for some time and none knew if he were alive or dead.

Just then Macduff entered, clutching by the hair Macbeth's bruised and battered head. Blood still dripped from where it had been severed from his body.

"Hail, King!" he cried to Malcolm, holding his trophy high, "Hail, King of Scotland!"

CHARACTERS IN THE PLAY

DUNCAN King of Scotland

MALCOLM Duncan's elder son

DONALBAIN Duncan's younger son

MACBETH General of the Scottish army, Thane of Glamis

LADY MACBETH Macbeth's wife

BANQUO General of the Scottish army

FLEANCE Banquo's son

MACDUFF Scottish nobleman, Thane of Fife

LADY MACDUFF Macduff's wife

YOUNG MACDUFF Macduff's son

ROSS Scottish nobleman, Thane of Ross

LENNOX Scottish nobleman

MENTEITH Scottish nobleman

ANGUS Scottish nobleman

CAITHNESS Scottish nobleman

SIWARD Commander of the English army, Earl of Northumberland

YOUNG SIWARD Siward's son

THREE WITCHES	who stir up trouble with their predictions
HECATE	Goddess of all witches
THREE MURDERERS	who murder Banquo and Macduff's family
PORTER	who makes jokes and drinks too much
SEYTON	Macbeth's armorer
ENGLISH DOCTOR	who tells of the English king's power to cure disease
SCOTTISH DOCTOR	who Macbeth employs to cure his wife's madness
GENTLEWOMAN	Lady Macbeth's maidservant
SERGEANT	who gives Duncan a report of the battle
OLD MAN	who talks with Ross
LORD	who talks with Lennox
1ST APPARITION	A head in a helmet
2ND APPARITION	A newborn baby
3RD APPARITION	A crowned child with a tree in its hand

Lords
Messengers
Soldiers
Servants
Attendants

ACT 1

ACT 1 SCENE 1
THREE WITCHES PLAN TO MEET
MACBETH AFTER A BATTLE. THEIR
FAMILIAR SPIRITS, GRAYMALKIN AND
PADDOCK, CALL THEM AWAY AND THEY
LEAVE, SPEAKING OMINOUS WORDS.

> **DISK LINK**
> Before you read farther, why
> not find out who's who in
> MEET THE CHARACTERS?

SCENE 1
A desolate place

Thunder and lightning. Enter three WITCHES

FIRST WITCH
　When shall we three meet again
　In thunder, lightning, or in rain?
SECOND WITCH
　When the hurlyburly's done,
　When the battle's lost and won.
THIRD WITCH
　That will be ere the set of sun.
FIRST WITCH
　Where the place?
SECOND WITCH
　　　　　　　　　Upon the heath.
THIRD WITCH
　There to meet with Macbeth.
FIRST WITCH
　I come, Graymalkin!
SECOND WITCH
　Paddock calls.
THIRD WITCH
　Anon.
ALL
　Fair is foul, and foul is fair:
　Hover through the fog and filthy air.

Exeunt

ACT 1 SCENE 2
A WOUNDED SERGEANT TELLS KING
DUNCAN THAT MACBETH HAS KILLED
THE REBEL MACDONWALD BUT THERE HAS
BEEN AN ATTACK BY FRESH NORWEGIAN
TROOPS. ROSS LATER REPORTS THAT
MACBETH AND BANQUO HAVE BEATEN
THE NORWEGIANS AND THE SCOTTISH
TRAITOR THE THANE OF CAWDOR.
DUNCAN SENTENCES CAWDOR TO
DEATH AND ANNOUNCES THAT HE
WILL GIVE HIS TITLE TO MACBETH.

SCENE 2
A camp near Forres

Trumpet calls. Enter KING DUNCAN, MALCOLM, DONALBAIN,
LENNOX, *with Attendants, meeting a wounded* SERGEANT

DUNCAN
　What bloody man is that? He can report,
　As seemeth by his plight, of the revolt
　The newest state.

MALCOLM

                This is the sergeant
Who like a good and hardy soldier fought
'Gainst my captivity. Hail, brave friend!
Say to the king the knowledge of the broil
As thou didst leave it.

SERGEANT

                 Doubtful it stood;
As two spent swimmers, that do cling together
And choke their art. The merciless Macdonwald
(Worthy to be a rebel, for to that
The multiplying villainies of nature
Do swarm upon him) from the western isles
Of kerns and gallowglasses is supplied;
And fortune, on his damnèd quarrel smiling,
Showed like a rebel's whore. But all's too weak;
For brave Macbeth (well he deserves that name)
Disdaining fortune, with his brandished steel,
Which smoked with bloody execution,
Like valour's minion carved out his passage
Till he faced the slave,
Which ne'er shook hands, nor bade farewell to him,
Till he unseamed him from the nave to the chaps,
And fixed his head upon our battlements.

DUNCAN

O valiant cousin! worthy gentleman!

SERGEANT

As whence the sun 'gins his reflection
Shipwrecking storms and direful thunders break,
So from that spring whence comfort seemed to come,
Discomfort swells. Mark, King of Scotland, mark.
No sooner justice had with valour armed
Compelled these skipping kerns to trust their heels,
But the Norwegian lord surveying vantage,
With furbished arms and new supplies of men
Began a fresh assault.

DUNCAN

               Dismayed not this
Our captains, Macbeth and Banquo?

SERGEANT

                      Yes;
As sparrows eagles, or the hare the lion.
If I say sooth, I must report they were
As cannons overcharged with double cracks,

So they
Doubly redoubled strokes upon the foe.
Except they meant to bathe in reeking wounds,
Or memorize another Golgotha,
I cannot tell—
But I am faint, my gashes cry for help.

DUNCAN
So well thy words become thee as thy wounds;
They smack of honour both. Go get him surgeons.

Exit SERGEANT, *attended*

Enter ROSS

Who comes here?

MALCOLM
                    The worthy Thane of Ross.

LENNOX
What a haste looks through his eyes! So should he look
That seems to speak things strange.

ROSS
                              God save the king!

DUNCAN
Whence camest thou, worthy Thane?

ROSS
                                From Fife, great King;
Where the Norwegian banners flout the sky
And fan our people cold.
Norway himself, with terrible numbers,
Assisted by that most disloyal traitor
The Thane of Cawdor, began a dismal conflict;
Till that Bellona's bridegroom, lapped in proof,
Confronted him with self-comparisons,
Point against point, rebellious arm 'gainst arm,
Curbing his lavish spirit; and, to cònclude,
The victory fell on us.

DUNCAN
                    Great happiness!

ROSS
That now Sweno,
The Norways' king, craves composition;
Nor would we deign him burial of his men
Till he disbursèd at Saint Colme's Inch
Ten thousand dollars to our general use.

DUNCAN

No more that Thane of Cawdor shall deceive
Our bosom interest: go pronounce his
    present death,
And with his former title greet Macbeth.

ROSS

I'll see it done.

DUNCAN

What he hath lost noble Macbeth hath won.

Exeunt

SCENE 3
A heath near Forres

ACT 1 SCENE 3
THE WITCHES TELL MACBETH THAT HE IS THANE OF CAWDOR AND WILL BE KING OF SCOTLAND. THEY TELL BANQUO THAT HE WILL BE THE FATHER OF FUTURE KINGS. ROSS BRINGS THE MEN A MESSAGE FROM DUNCAN CONFIRMING THAT MACBETH HAS INDEED BEEN MADE THANE OF CAWDOR.

DISK LINK
Can you remember all the characters, props, and sound effects in this scene? Test yourself in MAKE A SCENE.

Thunder. Enter the three WITCHES

FIRST WITCH

Where hast thou been, sister?

SECOND WITCH

Killing swine.

THIRD WITCH

Sister, where thou?

FIRST WITCH

A sailor's wife had chestnuts in her lap,
And munched, and munched, and munched.
    "Give me," quoth I.
"Aroint thee, witch!" the rump-fed ronyon cries.
Her husband's to Aleppo gone, master o' the Tiger;
But in a sieve I'll thither sail,
And, like a rat without a tail,
I'll do, I'll do, and I'll do.

SECOND WITCH

I'll give thee a wind.

FIRST WITCH

Thou'rt kind.

THIRD WITCH

And I another.

FIRST WITCH

I myself have all the other,
And the very ports they blow,
All the quarters that they know

I' the shipman's card.
I will drain him dry as hay.
Sleep shall neither night nor day
Hang upon his penthouse lid.
He shall live a man forbid.
Weary sev'n-nights, nine times nine
Shall he dwindle, peak, and pine.
Though his bark cannot be lost,
Yet it shall be tempest-tossed.
Look what I have.

SECOND WITCH

Show me, show me.

FIRST WITCH

Here I have a pilot's thumb,
Wrecked as homeward he did come.

Drum within

THIRD WITCH

A drum, a drum!
Macbeth doth come.

ALL

The weird sisters, hand in hand,
Posters of the sea and land,
Thus do go about, about,
Thrice to thine and thrice to mine
And thrice again, to make up nine.
Peace! the charm's wound up.

Enter MACBETH *and* BANQUO

MACBETH

So foul and fair a day I have not seen.

BANQUO

How far is't called to Forres? (*He sees the* WITCHES)
    What are these
So withered and so wild in their attire,
That look not like the inhabitants o' the earth,
And yet are on't? (*To the* WITCHES) Live you? or
    are you aught
That man may question? You seem to understand me,
By each at once her choppy finger laying
Upon her skinny lips. You should be women,
And yet your beards forbid me to interpret

That you are so.

MACBETH

                Speak, if you can. What are you?

FIRST WITCH

All hail, Macbeth, hail to thee, Thane of Glamis!

SECOND WITCH

All hail, Macbeth, hail to thee, Thane of Cawdor!

THIRD WITCH

All hail, Macbeth, that shalt be king hereafter!

BANQUO

(*To* MACBETH) Good Sir, why do you start and seem to fear
Things that do sound so fair? (*To the* WITCHES) I' the name
    of truth,
Are ye fantastical, or that indeed
Which outwardly ye show? My noble partner
You greet with present grace and great prediction
Of noble having and of royal hope,
That he seems rapt withal: to me you speak not.
If you can look into the seeds of time,
And say which grain will grow and which will not,
Speak then to me, who neither beg nor fear
Your favours nor your hate.

FIRST WITCH

Hail!

SECOND WITCH

Hail!

THIRD WITCH

Hail!

FIRST WITCH

Lesser than Macbeth, and greater.

SECOND WITCH

Not so happy, yet much happier.

THIRD WITCH

Thou shalt get kings, though thou be none.
So all hail, Macbeth and Banquo!

FIRST WITCH

Banquo and Macbeth, all hail!

MACBETH

Stay, you imperfect speakers, tell me more:
By Sinel's death I know I am Thane of Glamis;
But how of Cawdor? The Thane of Cawdor lives,
A prosperous gentleman; and to be king
Stands not within the prospect of belief,
No more than to be Cawdor. Say from whence

You owe this strange intelligence, or why
Upon this blasted heath you stop our way
With such prophetic greeting? Speak, I charge you.

                                        WITCHES *vanish*

BANQUO

The earth hath bubbles, as the water has,
And these are of them. Whither are they vanished?

MACBETH

Into the air; and what seemed corporal melted
As breath into the wind. Would they had stayed!

BANQUO

Were such things here as we do speak about?
Or have we eaten on the insane root
That takes the reason prisoner?

MACBETH

Your children shall be kings.

BANQUO

                                        You shall be king.

MACBETH

And Thane of Cawdor too. Went it not so?

BANQUO

To the selfsame tune and words. Who's here?

Enter ROSS *and* ANGUS

ROSS

The king hath happily received, Macbeth,
The news of thy success; and when he reads
Thy personal venture in the rebels' fight,
His wonders and his praises do contend
Which should be thine or his. Silenced with that,
In viewing o'er the rest o' the selfsame day,
He finds thee in the stout Norwegian ranks,
Nothing afeard of what thyself didst make,
Strange images of death. As thick as hail
Came post with post and every one did bear
Thy praises in his kingdom's great defence,
And poured them down before him.

ANGUS

                                        We are sent
To give thee from our royal master thanks;
Only to herald thee into his sight,
Not pay thee.

ROSS

And, for an earnest of a greater honour,
He bade me, from him, call thee Thane of Cawdor;
In which addition, hail, most worthy Thane!
For it is thine.

BANQUO

What! can the devil speak true?

MACBETH

The Thane of Cawdor lives. Why do you dress me
In borrowed robes?

ANGUS

Who was the thane lives yet,
But under heavy judgment bears that life
Which he deserves to lose. Whether he was combined
With those of Norway, or did line the rebel
With hidden help and vantage, or that with both
He laboured in his country's wreck, I know not;
But treasons capital, confessed and proved,
Have overthrown him.

MACBETH

(*Aside*) Glamis, and Thane of Cawdor!
The greatest is behind. (*To* ROSS *and* ANGUS) Thanks
    for your pains.
(*To* BANQUO) Do you not hope your children shall be kings,
When those that gave the Thane of Cawdor to me
Promised no less to them?

BANQUO

That, trusted home,
Might yet enkindle you unto the crown,
Besides the Thane of Cawdor. But 'tis strange!
And oftentimes, to win us to our harm,
The instruments of darkness tell us truths,
Win us with honest trifles, to betray 's
In deepest consequence.
(*To* ROSS *and* ANGUS) Cousins, a word, I pray you.

MACBETH

(*Aside*) Two truths
    are told,
As happy prologues to the swelling act
Of the imperial theme. (*To* ROSS *and* ANGUS) I thank you,
    gentlemen.
(*Aside*) This supernatural soliciting
Cannot be ill, cannot be good. If ill,
Why hath it given me earnest of success,

DISK LINK
There's a quotation on this page that will help you play WHO SAID WHAT?

Commencing in a truth? I am Thane of Cawdor.
If good, why do I yield to that suggestion
Whose horrid image doth unfix my hair
And make my seated heart knock at my ribs,
Against the use of nature? Present fears
Are less than horrible imaginings.
My thought, whose murder yet is but fantastical,
Shakes so my single state of man that function
Is smothered in surmise, and nothing is
But what is not.

BANQUO

(*To* ROSS *and* ANGUS) Look, how our partner's rapt.

MACBETH

(*Aside*) If chance will have me king, why, chance
    may crown me,
Without my stir.

BANQUO

             New honours come upon him,
Like our strange garments, cleave not to their mould
But with the aid of use.

MACBETH

             (*Aside*) Come what come may,
Time and the hour runs through the roughest day.

BANQUO

Worthy Macbeth, we stay upon your leisure.

MACBETH

(*To* ROSS *and* ANGUS) Give me your favour. My dull brain
    was wrought
With things forgotten. Kind gentlemen, your pains
Are registered where every day I turn
The leaf to read them. Let us toward the king.
(*To* BANQUO) Think upon what hath chanced, and,
    at more time,
The interim having weighed it, let us speak
Our free hearts each to other.

BANQUO

                 Very gladly.

MACBETH

Till then, enough. Come, friends.

Exeunt

THE THANE OF CAWDOR HAS BEEN
EXECUTED. DUNCAN REFLECTS THAT IT
IS IMPOSSIBLE TO JUDGE ANYONE BY
APPEARANCES. MACBETH DECLARES
HIS LOYALTY TO DUNCAN, WHO THEN
ANNOUNCES THAT HIS SON, MALCOLM,
IS HIS CHOSEN HEIR TO THE THRONE.
MACBETH SEES THIS AS AN OBSTACLE
TO HIS BECOMING KING AND BEGINS
TO THINK ABOUT HOW TO MAKE THE
WITCHES' PROPHECY COME TRUE.

SCENE 4
The Palace at Forres

Flourish. Enter KING DUNCAN, MALCOLM, DONALBAIN,
LENNOX, *and Attendants*

DUNCAN
    Is execution done on Cawdor? Are not
    Those in commission yet returned?

MALCOLM
                          My liege,
    They are not yet come back. But I have spoke
    With one that saw him die who did report
    That very frankly he confessed his treasons,
    Implored your highness' pardon and set forth
    A deep repentance. Nothing in his life
    Became him like the leaving it; he died
    As one that had been studied in his death
    To throw away the dearest thing he owed,
    As 'twere a careless trifle.

DUNCAN
                    There's no art
    To find the mind's construction in the face.
    He was a gentleman on whom I built
    An absolute trust.

Enter MACBETH, BANQUO, ROSS, *and* ANGUS

    (*To* MACBETH) O worthiest cousin!
    The sin of my ingratitude even now
    Was heavy on me! Thou art so far before
    That swiftest wing of recompense is slow
    To overtake thee. Would thou hadst less deserved,
    That the proportion both of thanks and payment
    Might have been mine! Only I have left to say,
    More is thy due than more than all can pay.

MACBETH
    The service and the loyalty I owe,
    In doing it, pays itself. Your highness' part
    Is to receive our duties; and our duties
    Are to your throne and state, children and servants,
    Which do but what they should, by doing everything
    Safe toward your love and honour.

DUNCAN

Welcome hither.
I have begun to plant thee, and will labour
To make thee full of growing.
    Noble Banquo,
That hast no less deserved, nor must be known
No less to have done so, let me infold thee
And hold thee to my heart.

BANQUO

There if I grow,
The harvest is your own.

DUNCAN

My plenteous joys,
Wanton in fulness, seek to hide themselves
In drops of sorrow. (*To* ALL) Sons, kinsmen, thanes,
And you whose places are the nearest, know
We will establish our estate upon
Our eldest, Malcolm, whom we name hereafter
The Prince of Cumberland; which honour must
Not unaccompanied invest him only,
But signs of nobleness, like stars, shall shine
On all deservers. (*To* MACBETH) From hence
    to Inverness,
And bind us further to you.

MACBETH

The rest is labour, which is not used for you!
I'll be myself the harbinger and make joyful
The hearing of my wife with your approach;
So humbly take my leave.

DUNCAN

My worthy Cawdor!

MACBETH

(*Aside*) The Prince of Cumberland! that is a step
On which I must fall down, or else o'erleap,
For in my way it lies. Stars, hide your fires!
Let not light see my black and deep desires.
The eye wink at the hand; yet let that be,
Which the eye fears, when it is done, to see.

Exit

DUNCAN

True, worthy Banquo; he is full so valiant,
And in his commendations I am fed;

It is a banquet to me. Let's after him,
Whose care is gone before to bid us welcome.
It is a peerless kinsman.

Fanfare. Exeunt

SCENE 5
Macbeth's Castle in Inverness

Enter LADY MACBETH, *reading a letter*

ACT 1 SCENE 5
LADY MACBETH READS A LETTER FROM
HER HUSBAND ABOUT THE WITCHES'
PROPHECY AND MACBETH'S NEW TITLE.
LADY MACBETH IS CONCERNED THAT
HER HUSBAND IS TOO KIND TO MURDER
DUNCAN AND TAKE THE FASTEST ROUTE
TO THE THRONE. SHE CALLS ON EVIL
SPIRITS TO ASSIST HER IN HER PLANS
TO KILL THE KING. WHEN MACBETH
ARRIVES, SHE TELLS HIM THAT SHE
WILL ARRANGE THE MURDER.

LADY MACBETH

(*Reads aloud*) "*They met me in the day of success; and
I have learned by the perfectest report, they have more
in them than mortal knowledge. When I burned in desire
to question them further, they made themselves air,
into which they vanished. Whiles I stood rapt in
the wonder of it, came missives from the king, who
all-hailed me, 'Thane of Cawdor'; by which title,
before, these weird sisters saluted me, and referred
me to the coming on of time, with, 'Hail, King that
shalt be!' This have I thought good to deliver
thee, my dearest partner of greatness, that thou
mightest not lose the dues of rejoicing, by being
ignorant of what greatness is promised thee. Lay
it to thy heart, and farewell.*"

Glamis thou art, and Cawdor, and shalt be
What thou art promised. Yet do I fear thy nature.
It is too full o' the milk of human kindness
To catch the nearest way. Thou wouldst be great;
Art not without ambition, but without
The illness should attend it. What thou wouldst highly,
That wouldst thou holily; wouldst not play false,
And yet wouldst wrongly win. Thou'dst have, great Glamis,
That which cries, "Thus thou must do," if thou have it;
And that which rather thou dost fear to do
Than wishest should be undone. Hie thee hither,
That I may pour my spirits in thine ear
And chastise with the valour of my tongue
All that impedes thee from the golden round
Which fate and metaphysical aid doth seem

DISK LINK

Test your knowledge of the play
in WALK-THROUGH MACBETH.
This quiz will sort the Thanes
from the Servants!

To have thee crowned withal.

Enter a SERVANT.

What is your tidings?

SERVANT

The king comes here tonight.

LADY MACBETH

Thou'rt mad to say it!
Is not thy master with him? who, were't so,
Would have informed for preparation.

SERVANT

So please you, it is true. Our thane is coming.
One of my fellows had the speed of him,
Who, almost dead for breath, had scarcely more
Than would make up his message.

LADY MACBETH

Give him tending;
He brings great news. (*Exit* SERVANT) The raven himself
    is hoarse
That croaks the fatal entrance of Duncan
Under my battlements. Come, you spirits
That tend on mortal thoughts, unsex me here,
And fill me from the crown to the toe, top-full
Of direst cruelty! Make thick my blood;
Stop up the access and passage to remorse,
That no compunctious visitings of nature
Shake my fell purpose nor keep peace between
The effect and it! Come to my woman's breasts,
And take my milk for gall, you murdering ministers,
Wherever in your sightless substances
You wait on nature's mischief! Come, thick night,
And pall thee in the dunnest smoke of hell,
That my keen knife see not the wound it makes,
Nor heaven peep through the blanket of the dark,
To cry, "Hold, hold!"

Enter MACBETH

Great Glamis! worthy Cawdor!
Greater than both, by the all-hail hereafter!
Thy letters have transported me beyond
This ignorant present, and I feel now
The future in the instant.

MACBETH

My dearest love,

Duncan comes here tonight.

LADY MACBETH

And when goes hence?

MACBETH

Tomorrow, as he purposes.

LADY MACBETH

O, never
Shall sun that morrow see!
Your face, my thane, is as a book where men
May read strange matters. To beguile the time,
Look like the time; bear welcome in your eye,
Your hand, your tongue; look like the innocent flower,
But be the serpent under't. He that's coming
Must be provided for; and you shall put
This night's great business into my dispatch;
Which shall to all our nights and days to come
Give solely sovereign sway and masterdom.

MACBETH

We will speak further.

LADY MACBETH

Only look up clear;
To alter favour ever is to fear.
Leave all the rest to me.

Exeunt

SCENE 6
Outside Macbeth's Castle

Music and torches. Enter KING DUNCAN, MALCOLM,
DONALBAIN, BANQUO, LENNOX, MACDUFF, ROSS, ANGUS,
and Attendants

DUNCAN

This castle hath a pleasant seat. The air
Nimbly and sweetly recommends itself
Unto our gentle senses.

BANQUO

This guest of summer,
The temple-haunting martlet, does approve,
By his loved mansionry, that the heaven's breath
Smells wooingly here. No jutty, frieze,

Buttress, nor coign of vantage, but this bird
Hath made his pendent bed and procreant cradle.
Where they most breed and haunt, I have observed,
The air is delicate.

Enter LADY MACBETH

DUNCAN
See, see, our honoured hostess!
(*To* LADY MACBETH) The love that follows us
sometime is our trouble,
Which still we thank as love. Herein I teach you
How you shall bid God yield us for your pains
And thank us for your trouble.

LADY MACBETH
All our service
In every point twice done and then done double
Were poor and single business to contend
Against those honours deep and broad wherewith
Your majesty loads our house. For those of old,
And the late dignities heaped up to them,
We rest your hermits.

DUNCAN
Where's the Thane of Cawdor?
We coursed him at the heels, and had a purpose
To be his purveyor; but he rides well,
And his great love, sharp as his spur, hath holp him
To his home before us. Fair and noble hostess,
We are your guest tonight.

LADY MACBETH
Your servants ever
Have theirs, themselves and what is theirs, in compt,
To make their audit at your highness' pleasure,
Still to return your own.

DUNCAN
Give me your hand;
Conduct me to mine host. We love him highly
And shall continue our graces towards him.
By your leave, hostess.

Exeunt

SCENE 7
Macbeth's Castle

ACT 1 SCENE 7

AFTER STRUGGLING WITH HIS CONSCIENCE, MACBETH DECIDES THAT HE WILL NOT COMMIT THE MURDER. HE TELLS LADY MACBETH BUT SHE CALLS HIM A COWARD AND QUESTIONS HIS MANLINESS. IN THIS WAY SHE PERSUADES HIM TO CHANGE HIS MIND AND EXPLAINS HOW SHE WILL MAKE DUNCAN'S BODYGUARDS DRUNK SO THAT THEY WILL BE BLAMED FOR THE KILLING.

Music and torches. Servants with dishes hurry across the stage. Then, enter MACBETH

MACBETH
> If it were done when 'tis done, then 'twere well
> It were done quickly. If the assassination
> Could trammel up the consequence, and catch
> With his surcease success; that but this blow
> Might be the be-all and the end-all here,
> But here, upon this bank and shoal of time,
> We'd jump the life to come. But in these cases
> We still have judgement here, that we but teach
> Bloody instructions, which, being taught, return
> To plague the inventor. This even-handed justice
> Commends the ingredients of our poisoned chalice
> To our own lips. He's here in double trust:
> First, as I am his kinsman and his subject,
> Strong both against the deed; then, as his host,
> Who should against his murderer shut the door,
> Not bear the knife myself. Besides, this Duncan
> Hath borne his faculties so meek, hath been
> So clear in his great office, that his virtues
> Will plead like angels, trumpet-tongued, against
> The deep damnation of his taking-off;
> And pity, like a naked new-born babe,
> Striding the blast, or heaven's cherubin, horsed
> Upon the sightless couriers of the air,
> Shall blow the horrid deed in every eye,
> That tears shall drown the wind. I have no spur
> To prick the sides of my intent, but only
> Vaulting ambition, which o'erleaps itself
> And falls on the other.

Enter LADY MACBETH

> How now! what news?

LADY MACBETH
> He has almost supped. Why have you left the chamber?

MACBETH
> Hath he asked for me?

DISK LINK
There's a quotation on this page that will help you play WHO SAID WHAT?

LADY MACBETH

Know you not he has?

MACBETH

We will proceed no further in this business.
He hath honoured me of late and I have bought
Golden opinions from all sorts of people,
Which would be worn now in their newest gloss,
Not cast aside so soon.

LADY MACBETH

Was the hope drunk
Wherein you dressed yourself? Hath it slept since?
And wakes it now, to look so green and pale
At what it did so freely? From this time
Such I account thy love. Art thou afeard
To be the same in thine own act and valour
As thou art in desire? Wouldst thou have that
Which thou esteem'st the ornament of life,
And live a coward in thine own esteem,
Letting "I dare not" wait upon "I would,"
Like the poor cat i' the adage?

MACBETH

Prithee, peace!
I dare do all that may become a man.
Who dares do more is none.

LADY MACBETH

What beast was't, then,
That made you break this enterprise to me?
When you durst do it, then you were a man;
And, to be more than what you were, you would
Be so much more the man. Nor time nor place
Did then adhere, and yet you would make both.
They have made themselves, and that their fitness now
Does unmake you. I have given suck, and know
How tender 'tis to love the babe that milks me.
I would, while it was smiling in my face,
Have plucked my nipple from his boneless gums,
And dashed the brains out, had I so sworn as you
Have done to this.

MACBETH

If we should fail?

LADY MACBETH

We fail?
But screw your courage to the sticking place,
And we'll not fail. When Duncan is asleep

(Whereto the rather shall his day's hard journey
Soundly invite him) his two chamberlains
Will I with wine and wassail so convince
That memory, the warder of the brain,
Shall be a fume, and the receipt of reason
A limbeck only. When in swinish sleep
Their drenchèd natures lie as in a death,
What cannot you and I perform upon
The unguarded Duncan? What not put upon
His spongy officers, who shall bear the guilt
Of our great quell?

MACBETH

              Bring forth men-children only;
For thy undaunted mettle should compose
Nothing but males. Will it not be received,
When we have marked with blood those sleepy two
Of his own chamber and used their very daggers,
That they have done't?

LADY MACBETH

              Who dares receive it other,
As we shall make our griefs and clamour roar
Upon his death?

MACBETH

              I am settled, and bend up
Each corporal agent to this terrible feat.
Away, and mock the time with fairest show;
False face must hide what the false heart doth know.

Exeunt

ACT 2

BANQUO AND HIS SON, FLEANCE,
ARE ON THEIR WAY TO BED. THEY
MEET MACBETH NERVOUSLY AWAITING
THE SIGNAL TO COMMIT THE MURDER.
BANQUO SAYS HE HAS DREAMED OF
THE WITCHES AND THE TWO MEN
AGREE TO DISCUSS THE PROPHECIES AT
A LATER DATE. AFTER THEY HAVE LEFT,
MACBETH HALLUCINATES. HE THINKS
HE CAN SEE A DAGGER COVERED IN
BLOOD HANGING IN MIDAIR IN FRONT
OF HIM. THEN A BELL RINGS, THE
SIGNAL FOR MACBETH TO ACT.

SCENE 1
The Court of Macbeth's Castle

Enter BANQUO*, and* FLEANCE *bearing a torch before him*

BANQUO
How goes the night, boy?

FLEANCE
The moon is down; I have not heard the clock.

BANQUO
And she goes down at twelve.

FLEANCE
I take't, 'tis later, Sir.

BANQUO
Hold, take my sword. There's husbandry in heaven;
Their candles are all out. Take thee that too.
A heavy summons lies like lead upon me,
And yet I would not sleep. Merciful powers,
Restrain in me the cursed thoughts that nature
Gives way to in repose!

Enter MACBETH*, and a Servant with a torch*

Give me my sword.
(*To* MACBETH) Who's there?

MACBETH
A friend.

BANQUO
What, Sir, not yet at rest? The king's a-bed.
He hath been in unusual pleasure, and
Sent forth great largess to your offices.
This diamond he greets your wife withal,
By the name of most kind hostess, and shut up
In measureless content.

MACBETH
Being unprepared,
Our will became the servant to defect,
Which else should free have wrought.

BANQUO
All's well.
I dreamt last night of the three weird sisters.
To you they have showed some truth.

MACBETH

I think not of them.
Yet, when we can entreat an hour to serve,
We would spend it in some words upon that business,
If you would grant the time.

BANQUO

At your kind'st leisure.

MACBETH

If you shall cleave to my consent, when 'tis,
It shall make honour for you.

BANQUO

So I lose none
In seeking to augment it but still keep
My bosom franchised and allegiance clear,
I shall be counselled.

MACBETH

Good repose the while!

BANQUO

Thanks, Sir. The like to you!

Exeunt BANQUO *and* FLEANCE

MACBETH

(*To the Servant*) Go bid thy mistress, when my drink is ready,
She strike upon the bell. Get thee to bed.

Exit Servant

Is this a dagger which I see before me,
The handle toward my hand? (*To the dagger*) Come, let me
clutch thee.
I have thee not, and yet I see thee still.
Art thou not, fatal vision, sensible
To feeling as to sight? or art thou but
A dagger of the mind, a false creation,
Proceeding from the heat-oppressèd brain?
I see thee yet, in form as palpable
As this which now I draw.
Thou marshall'st me the way that I was going,
And such an instrument I was to use.
Mine eyes are made the fools o' the other senses,
Or else worth all the rest. I see thee still,
And on thy blade and dudgeon gouts of blood,
Which was not so before. There's no such thing.
It is the bloody business which informs
Thus to mine eyes. Now o'er the one half-world

Nature seems dead, and wicked dreams abuse
The curtained sleep. Witchcraft celebrates
Pale Hecate's offerings, and withered murder,
Alarumed by his sentinel, the wolf,
Whose howl's his watch, thus with his stealthy pace.
With Tarquin's ravishing strides, towards his design
Moves like a ghost. Thou sure and firm-set earth,
Hear not my steps, which way they walk, for fear
Thy very stones prate of my whereabout,
And take the present horror from the time,
Which now suits with it. Whiles I threat, he lives;
Words to the heat of deeds too cold breath gives.

A bell rings

I go, and it is done. The bell invites me.
Hear it not, Duncan, for it is a knell
That summons thee to heaven or to hell.

Exit

ACT 2 SCENE 2

LADY MACBETH IS AWAITING MACBETH'S RETURN. SHE HAS DRUGGED THE GUARDS BUT WORRIES THAT MACBETH MAY NOT HAVE KILLED DUNCAN. MACBETH ARRIVES AND TELLS HER THAT HE HAS DONE THE DEED. HE SAYS THAT HE IS UNABLE TO SAY THE WORD "AMEN" AND HAS BEGUN TO HEAR IMAGINARY VOICES. LADY MACBETH TELLS HIM TO TAKE THE DAGGERS BACK TO THE GUARDS AND SMEAR THEIR FACES WITH BLOOD BUT HE REFUSES. SHE GOES HERSELF.

DISK LINK
Can you remember all the characters, props, and sound effects in this scene? Test yourself in MAKE A SCENE.

SCENE 2
In Macbeth's Castle, near Duncan's chamber

Enter LADY MACBETH

LADY MACBETH

That which hath made them drunk hath made me bold;
What hath quenched them hath given me fire.

Sound of an owl

Hark! Peace!
It was the owl that shrieked, the fatal bellman,
Which gives the stern'st good night. He is about it.
The doors are open, and the surfeited grooms
Do mock their charge with snores. I have drugged
    their possets,
That death and nature do contend about them
Whether they live or die.

MACBETH

(*Within*) Who's there? what, ho!

LADY MACBETH

Alack, I am afraid they have awaked,
And 'tis not done. The attempt and not the deed
Confounds us. Hark! I laid their daggers ready;
He could not miss 'em. Had he not resembled
My father as he slept, I had done't.

Enter MACBETH *with two bloody daggers*

My husband!

MACBETH

I have done the deed. Didst thou not hear a noise?

LADY MACBETH

I heard the owl scream and the crickets cry.
Did not you speak?

MACBETH

When?

LADY MACBETH

Now.

MACBETH

As I descended?

LADY MACBETH

Ay.

MACBETH

Hark! Who lies i' the second chamber?

LADY MACBETH

Donalbain.

MACBETH

(*Looking at his hands*) This is a sorry sight.

LADY MACBETH

A foolish thought, to say a sorry sight.

MACBETH

There's one did laugh in 's sleep, and one cried, "Murder!"
That they did wake each other. I stood and heard them.
But they did say their prayers and addressed them
Again to sleep.

LADY MACBETH

There are two lodged together.

MACBETH

One cried, "God bless us!" and, "Amen!" the other,
As they had seen me with these hangman's hands.
Listening their fear, I could not say, "Amen!"
When they did say, "God bless us!"

LADY MACBETH

Consider it not so deeply.

MACBETH

But wherefore could not I pronounce "Amen"?
I had most need of blessing, and "Amen"
Stuck in my throat.

LADY MACBETH

               These deeds must not be thought
After these ways. So, it will make us mad.

MACBETH

Methought I heard a voice cry, "Sleep no more!
Macbeth does murder sleep," the innocent sleep,
Sleep that knits up the ravelled sleave of care,
The death of each day's life, sore labour's bath,
Balm of hurt minds, great nature's second course,
Chief nourisher in life's feast.

LADY MACBETH

                  What do you mean?

MACBETH

Still it cried, "Sleep no more!" to all the house;
"Glamis hath murdered sleep, and therefore Cawdor
Shall sleep no more! Macbeth shall sleep no more!"

LADY MACBETH

Who was it that thus cried? Why, worthy Thane,
You do unbend your noble strength to think
So brainsickly of things. Go get some water,
And wash this filthy witness from your hand.
Why did you bring these daggers from the place?
They must lie there. Go carry them and smear
The sleepy grooms with blood.

MACBETH

                  I'll go no more.
I am afraid to think what I have done;
Look on't again I dare not.

LADY MACBETH

                Infirm of purpose!
Give me the daggers. The sleeping and the dead
Are but as pictures. 'Tis the eye of childhood
That fears a painted devil. If he do bleed,
I'll gild the faces of the grooms withal,
For it must seem their guilt.

Exit

Knocking within

DISK LINK
There's a quotation on this page that will help you play WHO SAID WHAT?

MACBETH

Whence is that knocking?
How is't with me, when every noise appals me?
What hands are here? Ha! they pluck out mine eyes.
Will all great Neptune's ocean wash this blood
Clean from my hand? No, this my hand will rather
The multitudinous seas incarnadine,
Making the green one red.

Re-enter LADY MACBETH

LADY MACBETH

My hands are of your colour; but I shame
To wear a heart so white. (*Knocking within*) I hear a knocking
At the south entry. Retire we to our chamber.
A little water clears us of this deed.
How easy is it, then! Your constancy
Hath left you unattended. (*Knocking within*) Hark! more
knocking.
Get on your nightgown, lest occasion call us,
And show us to be watchers. Be not lost
So poorly in your thoughts.

MACBETH

To know my deed, 'twere best not know myself.
(*Knocking within*)
Wake Duncan with thy knocking! I would thou couldst!

Exeunt

SCENE 3
The entrance to Macbeth's Castle

Knocking within. Enter a PORTER

ACT 2 SCENE 3

MACBETH'S PORTER PRETENDS TO BE THE KEEPER OF HELL'S GATE AND IMAGINES WHAT CHARACTERS MIGHT BE KNOCKING. EVENTUALLY, HE LETS IN LENNOX AND MACDUFF AND TALKS TO THEM ABOUT THE EFFECTS OF DRINKING. MACDUFF GOES TO WAKE THE KING AND SHOUTS OUT THE HORRIFIC NEWS. MACBETH KILLS THE GUARDS, CLAIMING THAT THEY MUST BE TO BLAME. DUNCAN'S SONS, MALCOLM AND DONALBAIN, REALIZE THAT THEIR OWN LIVES ARE IN DANGER AND DECIDE TO LEAVE THE COUNTRY.

PORTER

Here's a knocking indeed! If a man were porter of hell gate, he should have old turning the key. (*Knocking within*) Knock, knock, knock! Who's there, i' the name of Beelzebub? Here's a farmer that hanged himself on the expectation of plenty. Come in time-server; have napkins enough about you; here you'll sweat for't. (*Knocking within*) Knock, knock! Who's there, in the other devil's name? Faith, here's an equivocator, that could swear in both the scales against either scale; who committed treason enough for God's sake, yet could not equivocate to heaven. O, come in, equivocator. (*Knocking within*) Knock, knock, knock! Who's there? Faith, here's an English tailor come hither, for stealing out of a French hose. Come in, tailor. Here you may roast your goose. (*Knocking within*) Knock, knock; never at quiet! What are you? But this place is too cold for hell. I'll devil-porter it no further. I had thought to have let in some of all professions that go the primrose way to the everlasting bonfire. (*Knocking within*) Anon, anon! I pray you, remember the porter.

Opens the door
Enter MACDUFF *and* LENNOX

MACDUFF

Was it so late, friend, ere you went to bed, that you do lie so late?

PORTER

Faith Sir, we were carousing till the second cock; and drink, Sir, is a great provoker of three things.

MACDUFF

What three things does drink especially provoke?

PORTER

Marry, Sir, nose-painting, sleep, and urine. Lechery, Sir, it provokes, and unprovokes: it provokes the desire, but it takes away the performance. Therefore, much drink may be said to be an equivocator with lechery: it makes him, and it mars him; it sets him on, and it takes him off; it persuades him, and disheartens him; makes him stand to, and not stand to; in conclusion, equivocates him in a sleep, and, giving him the lie, leaves him.

MACDUFF

I believe drink gave thee the lie last night.

PORTER

That it did, Sir, i' the very throat on me; but I requited him for his lie; and, I think, being too strong for him, though he took up my legs sometime, yet I made a shift to cast him.

MACDUFF

Is thy master stirring?

Enter MACBETH

Our knocking has awaked him; here he comes.

LENNOX

(*To* MACBETH) Good morrow, noble Sir.

MACBETH

Good morrow, both.

MACDUFF

Is the king stirring, worthy Thane?

MACBETH

Not yet.

MACDUFF

He did command me to call timely on him;
I have almost slipped the hour.

MACBETH

I'll bring you to him.

MACDUFF

I know this is a joyful trouble to you;
But yet 'tis one.

MACBETH

The labour we delight in physics pain.
This is the door.

MACDUFF

I'll make so bold to call,
For 'tis my limited service.

Exit

LENNOX

Goes the king hence today?

MACBETH

He does; he did appoint so.

LENNOX

The night has been unruly, where we lay,
Our chimneys were blown down; and, as they say,
Lamentings heard i' the air, strange screams of death,
And prophesying with accents terrible
Of dire combustion and confused events
New hatched to the woeful time. The obscure bird
Clamoured the livelong night. Some say, the earth
Was feverous and did shake.

MACBETH

'Twas a rough night.

LENNOX

My young remembrance cannot parallel
A fellow to it.

Re-enter MACDUFF

DISK LINK
Guess what Shakespeare's more difficult words and phrases mean in the GLOSSARY GAME.

MACDUFF
O horror! horror! horror! Tongue nor heart
Cannot conceive nor name thee!

MACBETH AND LENNOX
What's the matter?

MACDUFF
Confusion now hath made his masterpiece!
Most sacrilegious murder hath broke ope
The Lord's anointed temple and stole thence
The life o' the building!

MACBETH
                              What is't you say, the life?

LENNOX
Mean you his majesty?

MACDUFF
Approach the chamber, and destroy your sight
With a new Gorgon. Do not bid me speak.
See, and then speak yourselves.

Exeunt MACBETH *and* LENNOX

                    Awake, awake!
Ring the alarm-bell. Murder and treason!
Banquo and Donalbain! Malcolm awake!
Shake off this downy sleep, death's counterfeit,
And look on death itself! Up, up, and see
The great doom's image! Malcolm! Banquo!
As from your graves rise up, and walk like sprites
To countenance this horror! Ring the bell.

Bell rings
Enter LADY MACBETH

LADY MACBETH
What's the business,
That such a hideous trumpet calls to parley
The sleepers of the house? Speak, speak!

MACDUFF
                                        O gentle lady,
'Tis not for you to hear what I can speak!
The repetition, in a woman's ear,
Would murder as it fell.

Enter BANQUO

MACDUFF

O Banquo, Banquo,
Our royal master's murdered!

LADY MACBETH

Woe, alas!
What, in our house?

BANQUO

Too cruel anywhere.
Dear Duff, I prithee, contradict thyself,
And say it is not so.

Re-enter MACBETH *and* LENNOX

MACBETH

Had I but died an hour before this chance,
I had lived a blessed time; for, from this instant,
There's nothing serious in mortality;
All is but toys; renown and grace is dead;
The wine of life is drawn, and the mere lees
Is left this vault to brag of.

Enter MALCOLM *and* DONALBAIN

DONALBAIN

What is amiss?

MACBETH

You are, and do not know't:
The spring, the head, the fountain of your blood
Is stopped, the very source of it is stopped.

MACDUFF

Your royal father's murdered.

MALCOLM

O! by whom?

LENNOX

Those of his chamber, as it seemed, had done't:
Their hands and faces were all badged with blood;
So were their daggers, which unwiped we found
Upon their pillows.
They stared, and were distracted. No man's life
Was to be trusted with them.

MACBETH

O, yet I do repent me of my fury
That I did kill them.

MACDUFF

                 Wherefore did you so?

MACBETH

Who can be wise, amazed, temperate and furious,
Loyal and neutral, in a moment? No man.
The expedition of my violent love
Outrun the pauser, reason. Here lay Duncan,
His silver skin laced with his golden blood,
And his gashed stabs looked like a breach in nature
For ruin's wasteful entrance; there, the murderers,
Steeped in the colours of their trade, their daggers
Unmannerly breeched with gore. Who could refrain,
That had a heart to love and in that heart
Courage to make 's love known?

LADY MACBETH

                (*Fainting*) Help me hence, ho!

MACDUFF

Look to the lady.

MALCOLM

(*Aside to* DONALBAIN) Why do we hold our tongues,
That most may claim this argument for ours?

DONALBAIN

(*Aside to* MALCOLM) What should be spoken
Here, where our fate, hid in an auger-hole,
May rush and seize us? Let's away. Our tears
Are not yet brewed.

MALCOLM

(*Aside to* DONALBAIN) Nor our strong sorrow
Upon the foot of motion.

BANQUO

                  Look to the lady.

LADY MACBETH *is carried out*

And when we have our naked frailties hid,
That suffer in exposure, let us meet,
And question this most bloody piece of work,
To know it further. Fears and scruples shake us.
In the great hand of God I stand, and thence
Against the undivulged pretence I fight
Of treasonous malice.

MACDUFF

                 And so do I.

ALL

So all.

MACBETH

Let's briefly put on manly readiness
And meet i' the hall together.

ALL

Well contented.

Exeunt all but MALCOLM *and* DONALBAIN

MALCOLM

What will you do? Let's not consort with them.
To show an unfelt sorrow is an office
Which the false man does easy. I'll to England.

DONALBAIN

To Ireland, I. Our separated fortune
Shall keep us both the safer. Where we are,
There's daggers in men's smiles; the near in blood,
The nearer bloody.

MALCOLM

This murderous shaft that's shot
Hath not yet lighted, and our safest way
Is to avoid the aim. Therefore, to horse!
And let us not be dainty of leave-taking,
But shift away. There's warrant in that theft
Which steals itself, when there's no mercy left.

Exeunt

ACT 2 SCENE 4
ROSS AND AN OLD MAN SPEAK OF THE
UNNATURAL WEATHER AND STRANGE
EVENTS THAT SEEM TO MIRROR THE
MURDER OF DUNCAN. MACDUFF
ARRIVES AND ANNOUNCES THAT
MALCOLM AND DONALBAIN HAVE
LEFT AND ARE SUSPECTED OF THE
MURDER THEMSELVES. MACBETH HAS
BEEN ELECTED KING AND GONE TO
SCONE TO BE CROWNED.

SCENE 4
Outside Macbeth's Castle

Enter ROSS *and an* OLD MAN

OLD MAN

Threescore and ten I can remember well;
Within the volume of which time I have seen
Hours dreadful and things strange; but this sore night
Hath trifled former knowings.

ROSS

Ah, good father,
Thou seest, the heavens, as troubled with man's act,
Threaten his bloody stage. By the clock 'tis day,

And yet dark night strangles the travelling lamp.
Is't night's predominance, or the day's shame,
That darkness does the face of earth entomb,
When living light should kiss it?

OLD MAN

'Tis unnatural,
Even like the deed that's done. On Tuesday last,
A falcon, towering in her pride of place,
Was by a mousing owl hawked at and killed.

ROSS

And Duncan's horses (a thing most strange and certain)
Beauteous and swift, the minions of their race,
Turned wild in nature, broke their stalls, flung out,
Contending 'gainst obedience, as they would make
War with mankind.

OLD MAN

'Tis said they ate each other.

ROSS

They did so, to the amazement of mine eyes
That looked upon't.

Enter MACDUFF

Here comes the good Macduff.
How goes the world, Sir, now?

MACDUFF

Why, see you not?

ROSS

Is't known who did this more than bloody deed?

MACDUFF

Those that Macbeth hath slain.

ROSS

Alas, the day!
What good could they pretend?

MACDUFF

They were suborned.
Malcolm and Donalbain, the king's two sons,
Are stol'n away and fled, which puts upon them
Suspicion of the deed.

ROSS

'Gainst nature still!
Thriftless ambition, that wilt ravin up
Thine own life's means! Then 'tis most like
The sovereignty will fall upon Macbeth.

DISK LINK

Test your knowledge of the play
in WALK-THROUGH MACBETH.
This quiz will sort the Thanes
from the Servants!

MACDUFF

He is already named, and gone to Scone
To be invested.

ROSS

Where is Duncan's body?

MACDUFF

Carried to Colmekill,
The sacred storehouse of his predecessors,
And guardian of their bones.

ROSS

Will you to Scone?

MACDUFF

No, cousin, I'll to Fife.

ROSS

Well, I will thither.

MACDUFF

Well, may you see things well done there. Adieu!
Lest our old robes sit easier than our new!

ROSS

Farewell, father.

OLD MAN

God's benison go with you, and with those
That would make good of bad, and friends of foes!

Exeunt

ACT 3

ACT 3 SCENE 1
BANQUO EXPRESSES HIS BELIEF THAT
MACBETH HAS USED EVIL MEANS
TO BECOME KING. HE WONDERS
WHETHER THE WITCHES' PROPHECY
THAT HIS CHILDREN WILL INHERIT
THE CROWN WILL ALSO COME TRUE.
MACBETH INVITES BANQUO TO
DINNER, THEN MEETS A COUPLE OF
MURDERERS TO PLAN HOW BANQUO
AND FLEANCE WILL BE KILLED.

DISK LINK
There's a quotation on this
page that will help you play
WHO SAID WHAT?

SCENE 1
The Royal Palace at Forres

Enter BANQUO, *dressed for riding*

BANQUO
> Thou hast it now: king, Cawdor, Glamis, all,
> As the weird women promised, and, I fear,
> Thou playedst most foully for't. Yet it was said
> It should not stand in thy posterity,
> But that myself should be the root and father
> Of many kings. If there come truth from them
> (As upon thee, Macbeth, their speeches shine)
> Why, by the verities on thee made good,
> May they not be my oracles as well,
> And set me up in hope? But hush! no more.

Trumpet calls. Enter MACBETH, *as King,* LADY
MACBETH, *as Queen,* LENNOX, ROSS, *Lords, Ladies,*
and Attendants

MACBETH
> Here's our chief guest.

LADY MACBETH
>   If he had been forgotten,
> It had been as a gap in our great feast,
> And all thing unbecoming.

MACBETH
> (*To* BANQUO) Tonight we hold a solemn supper, Sir,
> And I'll request your presence.

BANQUO
>   Let your highness
> Command upon me, to the which my duties
> Are with a most indissoluble tie
> For ever knit.

MACBETH
> Ride you this afternoon?

BANQUO
>   Ay, my good lord.

MACBETH
> We should have else desired your good advice,
> (Which still hath been both grave and prosperous)

In this day's council; but we'll take tomorrow.
Is't far you ride?

BANQUO

As far, my lord, as will fill up the time
'Twixt this and supper. Go not my horse the better,
I must become a borrower of the night
For a dark hour or twain.

MACBETH

                                        Fail not our feast.

BANQUO

My lord, I will not.

MACBETH

We hear our bloody cousins are bestowed
In England and in Ireland, not confessing
Their cruel parricide, filling their hearers
With strange invention. But of that tomorrow,
When therewithal we shall have cause of state
Craving us jointly. Hie you to horse. Adieu,
Till you return at night. Goes Fleance with you?

BANQUO

Ay, my good lord. Our time does call upon 's.

MACBETH

I wish your horses swift and sure of foot,
And so I do commend you to their backs.
Farewell.

Exit BANQUO

Let every man be master of his time
Till seven at night. To make society
The sweeter welcome, we will keep ourself
Till supper time alone. While then, God be with you!

Exeunt all but MACBETH, *and an* ATTENDANT

Sirrah, a word with you. Attend those men
Our pleasure?

ATTENDANT

They are, my lord, without the palace gate.

MACBETH

Bring them before us.

Exit ATTENDANT

                        To be thus is nothing,
But to be safely thus. Our fears in Banquo
Stick deep; and in his royalty of nature

Reigns that which would be feared. 'Tis much he dares,
And, to that dauntless temper of his mind,
He hath a wisdom that doth guide his valour
To act in safety. There is none but he
Whose being I do fear; and, under him,
My genius is rebuked, as, it is said,
Mark Antony's was by Caesar. He chid the sisters
When first they put the name of king upon me,
And bade them speak to him. Then prophet-like,
They hailed him father to a line of kings.
Upon my head they placed a fruitless crown,
And put a barren sceptre in my gripe,
Thence to be wrenched with an unlineal hand,
No son of mine succeeding. If't be so,
For Banquo's issue have I filed my mind;
For them the gracious Duncan have I murdered;
Put rancours in the vessel of my peace
Only for them, and mine eternal jewel
Given to the common enemy of man,
To make them kings, the seed of Banquo kings!
Rather than so, come fate into the list.
And champion me to the utterance! Who's there?

Re-enter ATTENDANT, with two MURDERERS

(*To the* ATTENDANT) Now go to the door, and stay there
    till we call.

                                   Exit ATTENDANT

(*To the* MURDERERS) Was it not yesterday we spoke together?

FIRST MURDERER
It was, so please your highness.

MACBETH
                         Well then, now
Have you considered of my speeches? Know
That it was he in the times past which held you
So under fortune, which you thought had been
Our innocent self. This I made good to you
In our last conference, passed in probation with you,
How you were borne in hand, how crossed, the instruments,
Who wrought with them, and all things else that might
To half a soul and to a notion crazed
Say, "Thus did Banquo."

FIRST MURDERER

> You made it known to us.

MACBETH

> I did so, and went further, which is now
> Our point of second meeting. Do you find
> Your patience so predominant in your nature
> That you can let this go? Are you so gospelled
> To pray for this good man and for his issue,
> Whose heavy hand hath bowed you to the grave
> And beggared yours for ever?

FIRST MURDERER

> We are men, my liege.

MACBETH

> Ay, in the catalogue ye go for men,
> As hounds and greyhounds, mongrels, spaniels, curs,
> Shoughs, water-rugs and demi-wolves, are clept
> All by the name of dogs. The valued file
> Distinguishes the swift, the slow, the subtle,
> The housekeeper, the hunter, every one
> According to the gift which bounteous nature
> Hath in him closed; whereby he does receive
> Particular addition, from the bill
> That writes them all alike; and so of men.
> Now, if you have a station in the file,
> Not i' the worst rank of manhood, say it;
> And I will put that business in your bosoms,
> Whose execution takes your enemy off,
> Grapples you to the heart and love of us,
> Who wear our health but sickly in his life,
> Which in his death were perfect.

SECOND MURDERER

> I am one, my liege,
> Whom the vile blows and buffets of the world
> Have so incensed that I am reckless what
> I do to spite the world.

FIRST MURDERER

> And I another
> So weary with disasters, tugged with fortune,
> That I would set my life on any chance,
> To mend it, or be rid on't.

MACBETH

> Both of you
> Know Banquo was your enemy.

BOTH MURDERERS

True, my lord.

MACBETH

So is he mine; and in such bloody distance,
That every minute of his being thrusts
Against my near'st of life; and though I could
With bare-faced power sweep him from my sight
And bid my will avouch it, yet I must not,
For certain friends that are both his and mine,
Whose loves I may not drop, but wail his fall
Who I myself struck down. And thence it is,
That I to your assistance do make love,
Masking the business from the common eye
For sundry weighty reasons.

SECOND MURDERER

We shall, my lord,
Perform what you command us.

FIRST MURDERER

Though our lives—

MACBETH

Your spirits shine through you. Within this hour at most
I will advise you where to plant yourselves,
Acquaint you with the perfect spy o' the time,
The moment on't; for't must be done tonight,
And something from the palace; always thought
That I require a clearness; and with him,
To leave no rubs nor botches in the work,
Fleance his son, that keeps him company,
Whose absence is no less material to me
Than is his father's, must embrace the fate
Of that dark hour. Resolve yourselves apart;
I'll come to you anon.

BOTH MURDERERS

We are resolved, my lord.

MACBETH

I'll call upon you straight: abide within.

Exeunt MURDERERS

It is concluded. Banquo, thy soul's flight,
If it find heaven, must find it out tonight.

Exit

ACT 3 SCENE 2
LADY MACBETH ADVISES HER HUSBAND
NOT TO BROOD ON WHAT THEY HAVE
DONE, AND TO PUT ON A CHEERFUL
FACE AT DINNER THAT NIGHT. MACBETH
SAYS HE WILL. HE ALSO MENTIONS THE
FACT THAT BANQUO AND FLEANCE ARE
STILL ALIVE AND HINTS THAT HE IS
GOING TO TAKE ACTION BUT DOESN'T
SAY WHAT IT IS TO BE.

DISK LINK
Test your knowledge of the play
in WALK-THROUGH MACBETH.
This quiz will sort the Thanes
from the Servants!

SCENE 2
The Royal Palace

Enter LADY MACBETH *and a* SERVANT

LADY MACBETH
Is Banquo gone from court?

SERVANT
Ay, madam, but returns again tonight.

LADY MACBETH
Say to the king, I would attend his leisure
For a few words.

SERVANT
        Madam, I will.

Exit

LADY MACBETH
            Nought's had, all's spent,
Where our desire is got without content.
'Tis safer to be that which we destroy
Than by destruction dwell in doubtful joy.

Enter MACBETH

How now, my lord! why do you keep alone,
Of sorriest fancies your companions making,
Using those thoughts which should indeed have died
With them they think on? Things without all remedy
Should be without regard. What's done is done.

MACBETH
We have scotched the snake, not killed it.
She'll close and be herself, whilst our poor malice
Remains in danger of her former tooth.
But let the frame of things disjoint, both the
    worlds suffer,
Ere we will eat our meal in fear and sleep
In the affliction of these terrible dreams
That shake us nightly. Better be with the dead,
Whom we, to gain our place, have sent to peace,
Than on the torture of the mind to lie
In restless ecstasy. Duncan is in his grave;
After life's fitful fever he sleeps well.

Treason has done his worst. Nor steel, nor poison,
Malice domestic, foreign levy, nothing
Can touch him further.

LADY MACBETH

Come on,
Gentle my lord, sleek o'er your rugged looks;
Be bright and jovial among your guests tonight.

MACBETH

So shall I, love; and so, I pray, be you.
Let your remembrance apply to Banquo;
Present him eminence, both with eye and tongue—
Unsafe the while, that we
Must lave our honours in these flattering streams,
And make our faces vizards to our hearts,
Disguising what they are.

LADY MACBETH

You must leave this.

MACBETH

O, full of scorpions is my mind, dear wife!
Thou know'st that Banquo, and his Fleance, lives.

LADY MACBETH

But in them nature's copy's not eterne.

MACBETH

There's comfort yet; they are assailable;
Then be thou jocund. Ere the bat hath flown
His cloistered flight, ere to black Hecate's summons
The shard-borne beetle with his drowsy hums
Hath rung night's yawning peal, there shall be done
A deed of dreadful note.

LADY MACBETH

What's to be done?

MACBETH

Be innocent of the knowledge, dearest chuck,
Till thou applaud the deed. Come, seeling night,
Scarf up the tender eye of pitiful day,
And with thy bloody and invisible hand
Cancel and tear to pieces that great bond
Which keeps me pale! Light thickens,
And the crow makes wing to the rooky wood.
Good things of day begin to droop and drowse,
Whiles night's black agents to their preys do rouse.
Thou marvellest at my words; but hold thee still:
Things bad begun make strong themselves by ill.
So, prithee, go with me.

Exeunt

ACT 3 SCENE 3
A THIRD MURDERER HAS JOINED THE OTHER TWO. THEY KILL BANQUO BUT FLEANCE ESCAPES. THEY DECIDE TO RETURN TO THE PALACE AND TELL MACBETH WHAT HAS HAPPENED.

SCENE 3

A lonely place near the Palace

Enter three MURDERERS

FIRST MURDERER
But who did bid thee join with us?

THIRD MURDERER
                                        Macbeth.

SECOND MURDERER
He needs not our mistrust, since he delivers
Our offices and what we have to do
To the direction just.

FIRST MURDERER
(*To the* THIRD MURDERER) Then stand with us.
The west yet glimmers with some streaks of day.
Now spurs the lated traveller apace
To gain the timely inn, and near approaches
The subject of our watch.

THIRD MURDERER
                                    Hark! I hear horses.

BANQUO
(*Within*) Give us a light there, ho!

SECOND MURDERER
                                          Then 'tis he! The rest
That are within the note of expectation
Already are i' the court.

FIRST MURDERER
                                    His horses go about.

THIRD MURDERER
Almost a mile, but he does usually,
So all men do, from hence to the palace gate
Make it their walk.

Enter BANQUO *and* FLEANCE *with a torch*

SECOND MURDERER
                              A light, a light!

THIRD MURDERER
                                                'Tis he.

FIRST MURDERER
Stand to't.

BANQUO

(*To* FLEANCE) It will be rain tonight.

FIRST MURDERER

Let it come down.

They set upon BANQUO

BANQUO

O, treachery! Fly, good Fleance, fly, fly, fly!
Thou mayst revenge. (*To the* MURDERER) O slave!

Dies. FLEANCE *escapes*

THIRD MURDERER

Who did strike out the light?

FIRST MURDERER

Was't not the way?

THIRD MURDERER

There's but one down; the son is fled.

SECOND MURDERER

We have lost best half of our affair.

FIRST MURDERER

Well, let's away, and say how much is done.

Exeunt

SCENE 4

A hall in the Palace

ACT 3 SCENE 4
AT THE BANQUET, ONE OF THE
MURDERERS REPORTS TO MACBETH
WHO IS VERY WORRIED ABOUT FLEANCE
HAVING ESCAPED ALIVE. THEN MACBETH
SEES BANQUO'S GHOST AMONG THE
DINERS. HE LOSES ALL SELF-CONTROL
AND SHOUTS AT THE GHOST TO LEAVE
HIM ALONE, ALMOST GIVING AWAY
HIS GUILT. LADY MACBETH ASKS THE
GUESTS TO LEAVE. MACBETH IS IN A
DESPERATE STATE AND VOWS TO VISIT
THE WITCHES AND GAIN INFORMATION
ABOUT HIS FUTURE.

A banquet is prepared. Enter MACBETH, LADY MACBETH, ROSS, LENNOX, LORDS, *and Attendants*

LADY MACBETH *sits*

MACBETH

You know your own degrees; sit down: at first and last
The hearty welcome.

The LORDS *sit*

LORDS

Thanks to your majesty.

MACBETH

Ourself will mingle with society, and play the
humble host. Our hostess keeps her state, but
in best time we will require her welcome.

LADY MACBETH

Pronounce it for me, Sir, to all our friends; for my heart
speaks they are welcome.

FIRST MURDERER *appears at the door*

MACBETH

(*To* LADY MACBETH) See, they encounter thee with their
    hearts' thanks.
(*To the* LORDS) Both sides are even. Here I'll sit i' the midst.
Be large in mirth; anon we'll drink a measure
The table round. (*To the* MURDERER) There's blood
    upon thy face.

FIRST MURDERER

'Tis Banquo's then.

MACBETH

'Tis better thee without than he within.
Is he despatched?

FIRST MURDERER

My lord, his throat is cut. That I did for him.

MACBETH

Thou art the best o' the cut-throats! Yet he's good
That did the like for Fleance. If thou didst it,
Thou art the nonpareil.

FIRST MURDERER

                    Most royal Sir,
Fleance is 'scaped.

MACBETH

(*Aside*) Then comes my fit again. I had else
    been perfect,
Whole as the marble, founded as the rock,
As broad and general as the casing air.
But now I am cabined, cribbed, confined, bound in
To saucy doubts and fears. (*To the* MURDERER) But
    Banquo's safe?

FIRST MURDERER

Ay, my good lord. Safe in a ditch he bides,
With twenty trenchèd gashes on his head,
The least a death to nature.

MACBETH
> Thanks for that!
> There the grown serpent lies; the worm that's fled
> Hath nature that in time will venom breed,
> No teeth for the present. Get thee gone. Tomorrow
> We'll hear ourselves again.

Exit MURDERER

LADY MACBETH
> My royal lord,
> You do not give the cheer. The feast is sold
> That is not often vouched, while 'tis a-making,
> 'Tis given with welcome. To feed were best at home.
> From thence the sauce to meat is ceremony;
> Meeting were bare without it.

MACBETH
> Sweet remembrancer!
> Now, good digestion wait on appetite,
> And health on both!

LENNOX
> May it please your highness sit?

MACBETH
> Here had we now our country's honour roofed,
> Were the graced person of our Banquo present;

The GHOST OF BANQUO *enters, and sits in*
Macbeth's place

> Who may I rather challenge for unkindness
> Than pity for mischance!

ROSS
> His absence, Sir,
> Lays blame upon his promise. Please't your highness
> To grace us with your royal company?

MACBETH
> The table's full.

LENNOX
> Here is a place reserved, Sir.

MACBETH
> Where?

LENNOX
> Here, my good lord. (MACBETH *notices the* GHOST) What is't
> that moves your highness?

MACBETH
Which of you have done this?

LORDS
                                        What, my good lord?

MACBETH
(*To the* GHOST) Thou canst not say I did it.
        Never shake
Thy gory locks at me.

ROSS
Gentlemen, rise. His highness is not well.

LADY MACBETH
Sit, worthy friends. My lord is often thus,
And hath been from his youth. Pray you, keep seat.
The fit is momentary; upon a thought
He will again be well. If much you note him,
You shall offend him and extend his passion.
Feed, and regard him not. (*To* MACBETH) Are you a man?

MACBETH
Ay, and a bold one, that dare look on that
Which might appal the devil.

LADY MACBETH
                                        O proper stuff!
This is the very painting of your fear.
This is the air-drawn dagger which, you said,
Led you to Duncan. O, these flaws and starts
(Impostors to true fear) would well become
A woman's story at a winter's fire,
Authorized by her grandam. Shame itself!
Why do you make such faces? When all's done,
You look but on a stool.

MACBETH
(*To the* LORDS) Prithee, see there! behold! look! lo! how
        say you?
Why, what care I? (*To the* GHOST) If thou canst nod,
        speak too.
(*To the* LORDS) If charnel houses and our graves must send
Those that we bury back, our monuments
Shall be the maws of kites.

                                        GHOST OF BANQUO *vanishes*

LADY MACBETH
                                        What! quite unmanned in folly?

MACBETH
If I stand here, I saw him.

LADY MACBETH

                              Fie, for shame!

MACBETH

Blood hath been shed ere now, i' the olden time,
Ere human statute purged the gentle weal;
Ay, and since too, murders have been performed
Too terrible for the ear. The times have been,
That, when the brains were out, the man would die,
And there an end! But now they rise again,
With twenty mortal murders on their crowns,
And push us from our stools. This is more strange
Than such a murder is.

LADY MACBETH

                              My worthy lord,
Your noble friends do lack you.

MACBETH

                              I do forget.
Do not muse at me, my most worthy friends,
I have a strange infirmity, which is nothing
To those that know me. Come, love and health to all!
Then I'll sit down. Give me some wine, fill full.
I drink to the general joy of the whole table,
And to our dear friend Banquo, whom we miss.
Would he were here! To all, and him, we thirst,
And all to all.

LORDS

                              Our duties, and the pledge.

Re-enter GHOST OF BANQUO

MACBETH

(*To the* GHOST) Avaunt! and quit my sight! Let the earth
        hide thee!
Thy bones are marrowless, thy blood is cold;
Thou hast no speculation in those eyes
Which thou dost glare with!

LADY MACBETH

                              (*To the* LORDS) Think of this, good peers,
But as a thing of custom. 'Tis no other.
Only it spoils the pleasure of the time.

MACBETH

What man dare, I dare.
Approach thou like the rugged Russian bear,
The armed rhinoceros, or the Hyrcan tiger;

Take any shape but that, and my firm nerves
Shall never tremble. Or be alive again,
And dare me to the desert with thy sword.
If trembling I inhabit then, protest me
The baby of a girl. Hence, horrible shadow!
Unreal mockery, hence!

GHOST OF BANQUO vanishes

Why, so! Being gone,
I am a man again. Pray you, sit still.

LADY MACBETH

(*To* MACBETH) You have displaced the mirth, broke the
good meeting,
With most admired disorder.

MACBETH

Can such things be,
And overcome us like a summer's cloud,
Without our special wonder? You make me strange
Even to the disposition that I owe,
When now I think you can behold such sights,
And keep the natural ruby of your cheeks,
When mine is blanched with fear.

ROSS

What sights, my lord?

LADY MACBETH

(*To the* LORDS) I pray you, speak not. He grows worse
and worse;
Question enrages him. At once, good night.
Stand not upon the order of your going,
But go at once.

LENNOX

Good night, and better health
Attend his majesty!

LADY MACBETH

A kind good night to all!

Exeunt all but MACBETH and LADY MACBETH

MACBETH

It will have blood, they say; blood will have blood.
Stones have been known to move and trees to speak;
Augurs and understood relations have
By maggot-pies and choughs and rooks brought forth
The secret'st man of blood. What is the night?

DISK LINK

There's a quotation on this page that will help you play WHO SAID WHAT?

LADY MACBETH

Almost at odds with morning, which is which.

MACBETH

How say'st thou, that Macduff denies his person
At our great bidding?

LADY MACBETH

                      Did you send to him, Sir?

MACBETH

I hear it by the way; but I will send.
There's not a one of them but in his house
I keep a servant fee'd. I will tomorrow
(And betimes I will) to the weird sisters.
More shall they speak; for now I am bent to know,
By the worst means, the worst. For mine own good,
All causes shall give way. I am in blood
Stepped in so far that, should I wade no more,
Returning were as tedious as go o'er.
Strange things I have in head, that will to hand,
Which must be acted ere they may be scanned.

LADY MACBETH

You lack the season of all natures, sleep.

MACBETH

Come, we'll to sleep. My strange and self-abuse
Is the initiate fear that wants hard use.
We are yet but young in deed.

Exeunt

ACT 3 SCENE 5

HECATE, GODDESS OF WITCHCRAFT, TELLS THE THREE WITCHES THAT THEY SHOULD NOT HAVE SPOKEN TO MACBETH WITHOUT INVOLVING HER. SHE TELLS THEM TO MEET HER AGAIN ANOTHER TIME WHEN MACBETH WILL ASK FOR MORE INFORMATION.

SCENE 5

A heath

Thunder. Enter the three WITCHES*, meeting* HECATE

FIRST WITCH

Why, how now, Hecate! you look angrily.

HECATE

Have I not reason, beldams as you are,
Saucy and overbold? How did you dare
To trade and traffic with Macbeth
In riddles and affairs of death;
And I, the mistress of your charms,
The close contriver of all harms,

Was never called to bear my part,
Or show the glory of our art?
And, which is worse, all you have done
Hath been but for a wayward son,
Spiteful and wrathful, who, as others do,
Loves for his own ends, not for you.
But make amends now. Get you gone,
And at the pit of Acheron
Meet me i' the morning. Thither he
Will come to know his destiny.
Your vessels and your spells provide,
Your charms and everything beside.
I am for the air. This night I'll spend
Unto a dismal and a fatal end.
Great business must be wrought ere noon.
Upon the corner of the moon
There hangs a vaporous drop profound.
I'll catch it ere it come to ground;
And that distilled by magic sleights
Shall raise such artificial sprites
As by the strength of their illusion
Shall draw him on to his confusion.
He shall spurn fate, scorn death, and bear
His hopes 'bove wisdom, grace and fear;
And you all know, security
Is mortals' chiefest enemy.

Music and a song within: "Come away, come away," etc.

Hark! I am called. My little spirit, see,
Sits in a foggy cloud, and stays for me.

Exit

FIRST WITCH
Come, let's make haste. She'll soon be back again.

Exeunt

SCENE 6

The Castle of Lennox

ACT 3 SCENE 6
LENNOX IS NOW SUSPICIOUS OF
MACBETH. ANOTHER LORD TELLS HIM
ABOUT MALCOLM'S WARM WELCOME
BY THE ENGLISH KING, EDWARD THE
CONFESSOR. HE SAYS THAT MACDUFF
HAS GONE TO ENGLAND TO ASK KING
EDWARD TO SEND AN ARMY TO HELP
THEM OVERTHROW MACBETH.

Enter LENNOX *and another* LORD

LENNOX

My former speeches have but hit your thoughts,
Which can interpret further. Only, I say,
Things have been strangely borne. The gracious Duncan
Was pitied of Macbeth. Marry, he was dead!
And the right-valiant Banquo walked too late;
Whom, you may say, if't please you, Fleance killed,
For Fleance fled. Men must not walk too late.
Who cannot want the thought how monstrous
It was for Malcolm and for Donalbain
To kill their gracious father? damnèd fact!
How it did grieve Macbeth! Did he not straight
In pious rage the two delinquents tear,
That were the slaves of drink and thralls of sleep?
Was not that nobly done? Ay, and wisely too!
For 'twould have angered any heart alive
To hear the men deny't. So that, I say,
He has borne all things well; and I do think
That, had he Duncan's sons under his key
(As, an't please heaven, he shall not) they should find
What 'twere to kill a father. So should Fleance.
But, peace! for from broad words and 'cause he failed
His presence at the tyrant's feast, I hear
Macduff lives in disgrace. Sir, can you tell
Where he bestows himself?

LORD

                  The son of Duncan,
From whom this tyrant holds the due of birth,
Lives in the English court, and is received
Of the most pious Edward with such grace
That the malevolence of fortune nothing
Takes from his high respect. Thither Macduff
Is gone to pray the holy king, upon his aid
To wake Northumberland and warlike Siward;
That, by the help of these (with Him above
To ratify the work) we may again
Give to our tables meat, sleep to our nights,
Free from our feasts and banquets bloody knives,

Do faithful homage and receive free honours—
All which we pine for now. And this report
Hath so exasperate the king that he
Prepares for some attempt of war.

LENNOX

                                                   Sent he to Macduff?

LORD

He did; and with an absolute "Sir, not I,"
The cloudy messenger turns me his back,
And hums, as who should say, "You'll rue the time
That clogs me with this answer."

LENNOX

                                                 And that well might
Advise him to a caution, to hold what distance
His wisdom can provide. Some holy angel
Fly to the court of England and unfold
His message ere he come, that a swift blessing
May soon return to this our suffering country
Under a hand accursed!

LORD

                                      I'll send my prayers with him.

Exeunt

ACT 4

ACT 4 SCENE 1

MACBETH VISITS THE WITCHES AND DEMANDS THAT THEY ANSWER HIS QUESTIONS. THE WITCHES CALL UP THREE APPARITIONS THAT TELL HIM IN RIDDLES WHAT THE FUTURE HOLDS. MACBETH BELIEVES THE NEWS IS GOOD. HE THEN ASKS IF IT IS TRUE THAT BANQUO'S HEIRS WILL BE KINGS. TO HIS DISMAY, HE IS SHOWN A PARADE OF EIGHT KINGS AND BANQUO. THE WITCHES DISAPPEAR. MACBETH HEARS OF MACDUFF'S FLIGHT TO ENGLAND AND VOWS TO MURDER HIS FAMILY.

DISK LINK

Can you remember all the characters, props, and sound effects in this scene? Test yourself in MAKE A SCENE.

SCENE 1

A cavern. In the middle, a boiling cauldron

Thunder. Enter the three WITCHES

FIRST WITCH
　Thrice the brinded cat hath mewed.

SECOND WITCH
　Thrice and once the hedge-pig whined.

THIRD WITCH
　Harpier cries 'tis time, 'tis time.

FIRST WITCH
　Round about the cauldron go;
　In the poisoned entrails throw.
　Toad, that under cold stone
　Days and nights has thirty-one
　Sweltered venom sleeping got,
　Boil thou first i' the charmèd pot.

ALL
　Double, double toil and trouble;
　Fire burn and cauldron bubble.

SECOND WITCH
　Fillet of a fenny snake,
　In the cauldron boil and bake;
　Eye of newt and toe of frog,
　Wool of bat and tongue of dog,
　Adder's fork and blind-worm's sting,
　Lizard's leg and howlet's wing,
　For a charm of powerful trouble,
　Like a hell-broth boil and bubble.

ALL
　Double, double toil and trouble;
　Fire burn and cauldron bubble.

THIRD WITCH
　Scale of dragon, tooth of wolf,
　Witches' mummy, maw and gulf
　Of the ravined salt-sea shark,
　Root of hemlock digged i' the dark,
　Liver of blaspheming Jew,
　Gall of goat, and slips of yew
　Slivered in the moon's eclipse,
　Nose of Turk and Tartar's lips,
　Finger of birth-strangled babe

Ditch-delivered by a drab:
Make the gruel thick and slab.
Add thereto a tiger's chaudron,
For the ingredients of our cauldron.

ALL

Double, double toil and trouble;
Fire burn and cauldron bubble.

SECOND WITCH

Cool it with a baboon's blood,
Then the charm is firm and good.

Enter HECATE

HECATE

O well done! I commend your pains,
And every one shall share i' the gains.
And now about the cauldron sing
Live elves and fairies in a ring,
Enchanting all that you put in.

Music and a song: "Black spirits," etc.

HECATE *retires*

SECOND WITCH

By the pricking of my thumbs,
Something wicked this way comes. (*Knocking*)
Open, locks,
Whoever knocks!

Enter MACBETH

MACBETH

How now, you secret, black, and midnight hags!
What is't you do?

ALL WITCHES

A deed without a name.

MACBETH

I conjure you, by that which you profess,
Howe'er you come to know it, answer me.
Though you untie the winds and let them fight
Against the churches; though the yesty waves
Confound and swallow navigation up;
Though bladed corn be lodged and trees blown down;
Though castles topple on their warders' heads;

Though palaces and pyramids do slope
Their heads to their foundations; though the treasure
Of nature's germens tumble all together,
Even till destruction sicken—answer me
To what I ask you.

FIRST WITCH

Speak.

SECOND WITCH

Demand.

THIRD WITCH

We'll answer.

FIRST WITCH

Say, if thou'dst rather hear it from our mouths,
Or from our masters?

MACBETH

Call 'em; let me see 'em.

FIRST WITCH

Pour in sow's blood, that hath eaten
Her nine farrow; grease that's sweaten
From the murderer's gibbet, throw
Into the flame.

ALL WITCHES

Come, high or low;
Thyself and office deftly show!

Thunder. FIRST APPARITION: *an Armed Head*

MACBETH

Tell me, thou unknown power—

FIRST WITCH

He knows thy thought.
Hear his speech, but say thou nought.

FIRST APPARITION

Macbeth! Macbeth! Macbeth! beware Macduff;
Beware the Thane of Fife. Dismiss me. Enough.

Descends

MACBETH

Whate'er thou art, for thy good caution, thanks!
Thou hast harped my fear aright: but one word more—

FIRST WITCH

He will not be commanded. Here's another,
More potent than the first.

Thunder. SECOND APPARITION: *a Bloody Child*

SECOND APPARITION
Macbeth! Macbeth! Macbeth!

MACBETH
Had I three ears, I'd hear thee.

SECOND APPARITION
Be bloody, bold, and resolute; laugh to scorn
The power of man, for none of woman born
Shall harm Macbeth.

Descends

MACBETH
Then live, Macduff. What need I fear of thee?
But yet I'll make assurance double sure
And take a bond of fate. Thou shalt not live!
That I may tell pale-hearted fear it lies
And sleep in spite of thunder.

Thunder. THIRD APPARITION: *a Child Crowned, with a tree in his hand*

What is this
That rises like the issue of a king
And wears upon his baby-brow the round
And top of sovereignty?

ALL WITCHES
Listen, but speak not to't.

THIRD APPARITION
Be lion-mettled, proud, and take no care
Who chafes, who frets, or where conspirers are.
Macbeth shall never vanquished be until
Great Birnam Wood to high Dunsinane Hill
Shall come against him.

Descends

MACBETH
That will never be.
Who can impress the forest, bid the tree
Unfix his earth-bound root? Sweet bodements! Good!
Rebellious dead, rise never till the Wood
Of Birnam rise, and our high-placed Macbeth
Shall live the lease of nature, pay his breath

To time and mortal custom. Yet my heart
Throbs to know one thing. Tell me, if your art
Can tell so much: shall Banquo's issue ever
Reign in this kingdom?

ALL WITCHES

                              Seek to know no more.

MACBETH

I will be satisfied. Deny me this,
And an eternal curse fall on you! Let me know.

Music. The cauldron descends

Why sinks that cauldron? and what noise is this?

FIRST WITCH

Show!

SECOND WITCH

Show!

THIRD WITCH

Show!

ALL WITCHES

Show his eyes, and grieve his heart!
Come like shadows, so depart!

*A show of eight kings, the last with a glass in
his hand;* GHOST OF BANQUO *following*

MACBETH

(*To the first king*) Thou art too like the spirit of Banquo.
    Down!
Thy crown does sear mine eye-balls. (*To the second king*) And
    thy hair,
Thou other gold-bound brow, is like the first.
(*To the* WITCHES) A third is like the former. Filthy hags!
Why do you show me this? A fourth! Start, eyes!
What, will the line stretch out to the crack of doom?
Another yet! A seventh! I'll see no more.
And yet the eighth appears, who bears a glass
Which shows me many more; and some I see
That twofold balls and treble scepters carry.
Horrible sight! Now, I see, 'tis true;
For the blood-boltered Banquo smiles upon me,
And points at them for his. (APPARITIONS *vanish*)
    What, is this so?

DISK LINK
Test your knowledge of the play in WALK-THROUGH MACBETH. This quiz will sort the Thanes from the Servants!

FIRST WITCH

Ay, Sir, all this is so. But why
Stands Macbeth thus amazèdly?
Come, sisters, cheer we up his sprites,
And show the best of our delights.
I'll charm the air to give a sound
While you perform your antic round,
That this great king may kindly say,
Our duties did his welcome pay.

Music. The WITCHES *dance and then vanish, with* HECATE

MACBETH

Where are they? Gone? Let this pernicious hour
Stand aye accursèd in the calendar!
Come in, without there!

Enter LENNOX

LENNOX

What's your grace's will?

MACBETH

Saw you the weird sisters?

LENNOX

No, my lord.

MACBETH

Came they not by you?

LENNOX

No, indeed, my lord.

MACBETH

Infected be the air whereon they ride,
And damned all those that trust them! I did hear
The galloping of horse. Who was't came by?

LENNOX

'Tis two or three, my lord, that bring you word
Macduff is fled to England.

MACBETH

Fled to England!

LENNOX

Ay, my good lord.

MACBETH

(*Aside*) Time, thou anticipat'st my dread exploits.
The flighty purpose never is o'ertook

Unless the deed go with it; from this moment
The very firstlings of my heart shall be
The firstlings of my hand. And even now,
To crown my thoughts with acts, be it thought
    and done!
The castle of Macduff I will surprise,
Seize upon Fife, give to the edge o' the sword
His wife, his babes, and all unfortunate souls
That trace him in his line. No boasting like a fool!
This deed I'll do before this purpose cool.
But no more sights!— (*To* LENNOX) Where are these
    gentlemen?
Come, bring me where they are.

Exeunt

ACT 4 SCENE 2
LADY MACDUFF TALKS TO HER SON
ABOUT HIS FATHER GOING TO ENGLAND.
SHE FEELS ABANDONED AND BELIEVES
MACDUFF NO LONGER LOVES HER OR
HIS CHILDREN. MURDERERS ARRIVE AND
BRUTALLY SLAUGHTER LADY MACDUFF
AND HER CHILDREN.

SCENE 2
Macduff's Castle in Fife

Enter LADY MACDUFF, *her* SON, *and* ROSS

LADY MACDUFF
What had he done, to make him fly the land?
ROSS
You must have patience, madam.
LADY MACDUFF
                          He had none.
His flight was madness. When our actions do not,
Our fears do make us traitors.
ROSS
                    You know not
Whether it was his wisdom or his fear.
LADY MACDUFF
Wisdom? To leave his wife, to leave his babes,
His mansion and his titles in a place
From whence himself does fly? He loves us not,
He wants the natural touch. For the poor wren
(The most diminutive of birds) will fight,
Her young ones in her nest, against the owl.
All is the fear and nothing is the love,
As little is the wisdom, where the flight
So runs against all reason.

Ross

My dearest coz,

I pray you, school yourself. But for your husband,
He is noble, wise, judicious, and best knows
The fits o' the season. I dare not speak much further;
But cruel are the times, when we are traitors
And do not know ourselves; when we hold rumour
From what we fear, yet know not what we fear,
But float upon a wild and violent sea
Each way and move. I take my leave of you.
Shall not be long but I'll be here again.
Things at the worst will cease, or else climb upward
To what they were before. (*To her* SON) My pretty cousin,
Blessing upon you!

Lady Macduff

Father'd he is, and yet he's fatherless.

Ross

I am so much a fool, should I stay longer,
It would be my disgrace and your discomfort.
I take my leave at once.

Exit

Lady Macduff

(*To her* SON) Sirrah, your father's dead;

And what will you do now? How will you live?

Son

As birds do, mother.

Lady Macduff

What, with worms and flies?

Son

With what I get, I mean, and so do they.

Lady Macduff

Poor bird! thou'dst never fear the net nor lime,
The pitfall nor the gin.

Son

Why should I, mother? Poor birds they are not set for.
My father is not dead, for all your saying.

Lady Macduff

Yes, he is dead. How wilt thou do for a father?

Son

Nay, how will you do for a husband?

Lady Macduff

Why, I can buy me twenty at any market.

DISK LINK

Guess what Shakespeare's more difficult words and phrases mean in the GLOSSARY GAME.

SON

Then you'll buy 'em to sell again.

LADY MACDUFF

Thou speak'st with all thy wit; and yet, i' faith,
With wit enough for thee.

SON

Was my father a traitor, mother?

LADY MACDUFF

Ay, that he was.

SON

What is a traitor?

LADY MACDUFF

Why, one that swears and lies.

SON

And be all traitors that do so?

LADY MACDUFF

Every one that does so is a traitor and must be hanged.

SON

And must they all be hanged that swear and lie?

LADY MACDUFF

Every one.

SON

Who must hang them?

LADY MACDUFF

Why, the honest men.

SON

Then the liars and swearers are fools; for there are
liars and swearers enough to beat the honest men
and hang up them.

LADY MACDUFF

Now, God help thee, poor monkey!
But how wilt thou do for a father?

SON

If he were dead, you'd weep for him. If you
would not, it were a good sign that I should
quickly have a new father.

LADY MACDUFF

Poor prattler, how thou talk'st!

Enter a MESSENGER

MESSENGER

Bless you, fair dame! I am not to you known,
Though in your state of honour I am perfect.

I doubt some danger does approach you nearly.
If you will take a homely man's advice,
Be not found here. Hence, with your little ones.
To fright you thus, methinks, I am too savage;
To do worse to you were fell cruelty,
Which is too nigh your person. Heaven preserve you!
I dare abide no longer.

Exit

LADY MACDUFF
         Whither should I fly?
I have done no harm. But I remember now
I am in this earthly world, where to do harm
Is often laudable, to do good sometime
Accounted dangerous folly. Why then, alas,
Do I put up that womanly defence,
To say I have done no harm?

Enter MURDERERS

         What are these faces?
FIRST MURDERER
Where is your husband?
LADY MACDUFF
I hope, in no place so unsanctified
Where such as thou may'st find him.
FIRST MURDERER
         He's a traitor.
SON
Thou liest, thou shag-haired villain!
FIRST MURDERER
       What, you egg!

Stabbing him

Young fry of treachery!
SON
      He has killed me, mother.
Run away, I pray you!

Dies

Exit LADY MACDUFF, *crying "Murder!"*
Exeunt MURDERERS, *following her*

SCENE 3
The Palace of King Edward in England

Enter MALCOLM *and* MACDUFF

MALCOLM
Let us seek out some desolate shade, and there
Weep our sad bosoms empty.

MACDUFF
                  Let us rather
Hold fast the mortal sword, and like good men
Bestride our down-fall'n birthdom. Each new morn
New widows howl, new orphans cry, new sorrows
Strike heaven on the face, that it resounds
As if it felt with Scotland and yelled out
Like syllable of dolour.

MALCOLM
                 What I believe I'll wail,
What know believe, and what I can redress,
As I shall find the time to friend, I will.
What you have spoke, it may be so perchance.
This tyrant, whose sole name blisters our tongues,
Was once thought honest; you have loved him well.
He hath not touched you yet. I am young; but something
You may deserve of him through me, and wisdom
To offer up a weak, poor, innocent lamb
To appease an angry god.

MACDUFF
I am not treacherous.

MALCOLM
                But Macbeth is.
A good and virtuous nature may recoil
In an imperial charge. But I shall crave your pardon.
That which you are my thoughts cannot transpose.
Angels are bright still, though the brightest fell.
Though all things foul would wear the brows of grace,
Yet grace must still look so.

MACDUFF
                  I have lost my hopes.

MALCOLM
Perchance even there where I did find my doubts.
Why in that rawness left you wife and child,
Those precious motives, those strong knots of love,

Without leave-taking? I pray you,
Let not my jealousies be your dishonours,
But mine own safeties. You may be rightly just,
Whatever I shall think.

MACDUFF

                    Bleed, bleed, poor country!
Great tyranny! lay thou thy basis sure,
For goodness dare not check thee! Wear thou thy wrongs;
The title is affeered! Fare thee well, lord.
I would not be the villain that thou thinkest
For the whole space that's in the tyrant's grasp,
And the rich East to boot.

MALCOLM

                  Be not offended:
I speak not as in absolute fear of you.
I think our country sinks beneath the yoke,
It weeps, it bleeds, and each new day a gash
Is added to her wounds. I think withal
There would be hands uplifted in my right;
And here from gracious England have I offer
Of goodly thousands. But, for all this,
When I shall tread upon the tyrant's head
Or wear it on my sword, yet my poor country
Shall have more vices than it had before,
More suffer and more sundry ways than ever,
By him that shall succeed.

MACDUFF

                  What should he be?

MALCOLM

It is myself I mean; in whom I know
All the particulars of vice so grafted
That, when they shall be opened, black Macbeth
Will seem as pure as snow, and the poor state
Esteem him as a lamb, being compared
With my confineless harms.

MACDUFF

                    Not in the legions
Of horrid hell can come a devil more damned
In evils to top Macbeth.

MALCOLM

                  I grant him bloody,
Luxurious, avaricious, false, deceitful,
Sudden, malicious, smacking of every sin
That has a name. But there's no bottom, none,

In my voluptuousness. Your wives, your daughters,
Your matrons and your maids, could not fill up
The cistern of my lust, and my desire
All continent impediments would o'erbear
That did oppose my will. Better Macbeth
Than such a one to reign.

MACDUFF

Boundless intemperance
In nature is a tyranny. It hath been
The untimely emptying of the happy throne
And fall of many kings. But fear not yet
To take upon you what is yours. You may
Convey your pleasures in a spacious plenty,
And yet seem cold, the time you may so hoodwink.
We have willing dames enough. There cannot be
That vulture in you, to devour so many
As will to greatness dedicate themselves,
Finding it so inclined.

MALCOLM

With this there grows
In my most ill-composed affection such
A staunchless avarice that, were I king,
I should cut off the nobles for their lands,
Desire his jewels and this other's house,
And my more-having would be as a sauce
To make me hunger more, that I should forge
Quarrels unjust against the good and loyal,
Destroying them for wealth.

MACDUFF

This avarice
Sticks deeper, grows with more pernicious root
Than summer-seeming lust, and it hath been
The sword of our slain kings. Yet do not fear.
Scotland hath foisons to fill up your will,
Of your mere own. All these are portable,
With other graces weighed.

MALCOLM

But I have none: the king-becoming graces,
As justice, verity, temperance, stableness,
Bounty, perseverance, mercy, lowliness,
Devotion, patience, courage, fortitude,
I have no relish of them, but abound
In the division of each several crime,
Acting it many ways. Nay, had I power, I should

Pour the sweet milk of concord into hell,
Uproar the universal peace, confound
All unity on earth.

MACDUFF

O Scotland, Scotland!

MALCOLM

If such a one be fit to govern, speak.
I am as I have spoken.

MACDUFF

Fit to govern!
No, not to live. O nation miserable,
With an untitled tyrant bloody-sceptered,
When shalt thou see thy wholesome days again,
Since that the truest issue of thy throne
By his own interdiction stands accused,
And does blaspheme his breed? Thy royal father
Was a most sainted king; the queen that bore thee,
Oftener upon her knees than on her feet,
Died every day she lived. Fare thee well!
These evils thou repeat'st upon thyself
Have banished me from Scotland. O my breast,
Thy hope ends here!

MALCOLM

Macduff, this noble passion,
Child of integrity, hath from my soul
Wiped the black scruples, reconciled my thoughts
To thy good truth and honour. Devilish Macbeth
By many of these trains hath sought to win me
Into his power; and modest wisdom plucks me
From over-credulous haste; but God above
Deal between thee and me! for even now
I put myself to thy direction and
Unspeak mine own detraction, here abjure
The taints and blames I laid upon myself,
For strangers to my nature. I am yet
Unknown to woman, never was forsworn,
Scarcely have coveted what was mine own,
At no time broke my faith, would not betray
The devil to his fellow, and delight
No less in truth than life. My first false speaking
Was this upon myself. What I am truly,
Is thine and my poor country's to command.
Whither indeed, before thy here-approach,
Old Siward, with ten thousand warlike men,

Already at a point, was setting forth.
Now we'll together; and the chance of goodness
Be like our warranted quarrel! Why are you silent?

MACDUFF

Such welcome and unwelcome things at once
'Tis hard to reconcile.

Enter a DOCTOR

MALCOLM

                          Well, more anon.
(*To the* DOCTOR) Comes the king forth, I pray you?

DOCTOR

Ay, Sir; there are a crew of wretched souls
That stay his cure. Their malady convinces
The great assay of art; but at his touch,
Such sanctity hath heaven given his hand,
They presently amend.

MALCOLM

                      I thank you, doctor.

Exit DOCTOR

MACDUFF

What's the disease he means?

MALCOLM

                            'Tis called the evil:
A most miraculous work in this good king,
Which often, since my here-remain in England,
I have seen him do. How he solicits heaven,
Himself best knows; but strangely-visited people,
All swol'n and ulcerous, pitiful to the eye,
The mere despair of surgery, he cures,
Hanging a golden stamp about their necks,
Put on with holy prayers; and 'tis spoken,
To the succeeding royalty he leaves
The healing benediction. With this strange virtue,
He hath a heavenly gift of prophecy,
And sundry blessings hang about his throne
That speak him full of grace.

Enter ROSS

MACDUFF

                        See, who comes here?

MALCOLM

My countryman; but yet I know him not.

MACDUFF

My ever-gentle cousin, welcome hither.

MALCOLM

I know him now. Good God, betimes remove
The means that makes us strangers!

ROSS

                                    Sir, amen.

MACDUFF

Stands Scotland where it did?

ROSS

                            Alas, poor country!
Almost afraid to know itself. It cannot
Be called our mother, but our grave; where nothing,
But who knows nothing, is once seen to smile;
Where sighs and groans and shrieks that rend the air
Are made, not marked; where violent sorrow seems
A modern ecstasy. The dead man's knell
Is there scarce asked for who; and good men's lives
Expire before the flowers in their caps,
Dying or ere they sicken.

MACDUFF

                  O, relation
Too nice, and yet too true!

MALCOLM

                What's the newest grief?

ROSS

That of an hour's age doth hiss the speaker:
Each minute teems a new one.

MACDUFF

                  How does my wife?

ROSS

Why, well.

MACDUFF

        And all my children?

ROSS

                  Well too.

MACDUFF

The tyrant has not battered at their peace?

ROSS

No; they were well at peace when I did leave 'em.

MACDUFF

Be not a niggard of your speech. How goes't?

DISK LINK

There's a quotation on this page that will help you play WHO SAID WHAT?

ROSS

    When I came hither to transport the tidings,
    Which I have heavily borne, there ran a rumour
    Of many worthy fellows that were out;
    Which was to my belief witnessed the rather,
    For that I saw the tyrant's power afoot.
    Now is the time of help. Your eye in Scotland
    Would create soldiers, make our women fight,
    To doff their dire distresses.

MALCOLM

                    Be't their comfort
    We are coming thither. Gracious England hath
    Lent us good Siward and ten thousand men.
    An older and a better soldier none
    That Christendom gives out.

ROSS

                    Would I could answer
    This comfort with the like! But I have words
    That would be howled out in the desert air,
    Where hearing should not latch them.

MACDUFF

                    What concern they?
    The general cause? or is it a fee-grief
    Due to some single breast?

ROSS

                    No mind that's honest
    But in it shares some woe; though the main part
    Pertains to you alone.

MACDUFF

                    If it be mine,
    Keep it not from me, quickly let me have it.

ROSS

    Let not your ears despise my tongue for ever,
    Which shall possess them with the heaviest sound
    That ever yet they heard.

MACDUFF

                    Hum! I guess at it.

ROSS

    Your castle is surprised; your wife and babes
    Savagely slaughtered. To relate the manner
    Were, on the quarry of these murdered deer,
    To add the death of you.

MALCOLM

                    Merciful heaven!

(*To* MACDUFF) What, man! Ne'er pull your hat upon
    your brows.
Give sorrow words. The grief that does not speak
Whispers the o'er-fraught heart and bids it break.

MACDUFF

My children too?

ROSS

                    Wife, children, servants, all
That could be found.

MACDUFF

                    And I must be from thence!
My wife killed too?

ROSS

                I have said.

MALCOLM

                    Be comforted.
Let's make us medicines of our great revenge,
To cure this deadly grief.

MACDUFF

He has no children. All my pretty ones?
Did you say all? O hell-kite! All?
What, all my pretty chickens and their dam
At one fell swoop?

MALCOLM

                  Dispute it like a man.

MACDUFF

                        I shall do so;
But I must also feel it as a man.
I cannot but remember such things were,
That were most precious to me. Did heaven look on,
And would not take their part? Sinful Macduff!
They were all struck for thee! Naught that I am,
Not for their own demerits, but for mine,
Fell slaughter on their souls. Heaven rest them now!

MALCOLM

Be this the whetstone of your sword. Let grief
Convert to anger; blunt not the heart, enrage it.

MACDUFF

O, I could play the woman with mine eyes
And braggart with my tongue! But, gentle heavens,
Cut short all intermission. Front to front
Bring thou this fiend of Scotland and myself.
Within my sword's length set him. If he 'scape,
Heaven forgive him too!

MALCOLM

This tune goes manly.
Come, go we to the king; our power is ready;
Our lack is nothing but our leave. Macbeth
Is ripe for shaking, and the powers above
Put on their instruments. Receive what cheer you may.
The night is long that never finds the day.

Exeunt

ACT 5

ACT 5 SCENE 1
WALKING AND SPEAKING IN HER
SLEEP, LADY MACBETH UNKNOWINGLY
REVEALS HER GUILT TO A DOCTOR
AND A GENTLEWOMAN. SHE MIMES
WASHING HER HANDS TO TRY TO
REMOVE THE STAIN OF BLOOD SHE
BELIEVES SHE CAN SEE. IT IS CLEAR
THAT HER GUILT IS DRIVING HER INSANE.

DISK LINK
Can you remember all the
characters, props, and sound
effects in this scene? Test
yourself in MAKE A SCENE.

SCENE 1
A room in Macbeth's Castle at Dunsinane

Enter a DOCTOR *and Lady Macbeth's* GENTLEWOMAN

DOCTOR
I have two nights watched with you, but can perceive no
truth in your report. When was it she last walked?

GENTLEWOMAN
Since his majesty went into the field, I have seen her rise
from her bed, throw her nightgown upon her, unlock her
closet, take forth paper, fold it, write upon't, read it,
afterwards seal it, and again return to bed; yet all this while
in a most fast sleep.

DOCTOR
A great perturbation in nature, to receive at once the benefit
of sleep, and do the effects of watching! In this slumbery
agitation, besides her walking and other actual performances,
what, at any time, have you heard her say?

GENTLEWOMAN
That, Sir, which I will not report after her.

DOCTOR
You may to me, and 'tis most meet you should.

GENTLEWOMAN
Neither to you nor any one, having no witness to
confirm my speech.

Enter LADY MACBETH, *with a candle*

Lo you, here she comes! This is her very guise, and, upon my
life, fast asleep. Observe her; stand close.

DOCTOR
How came she by that light?

GENTLEWOMAN
Why, it stood by her. She has light by her continually.
'Tis her command.

DOCTOR
You see, her eyes are open.

GENTLEWOMAN
Ay, but their sense is shut.

DOCTOR
What is it she does now? Look, how she rubs her hands.

GENTLEWOMAN

It is an accustomed action with her, to seem thus washing her hands. I have known her continue in this a quarter of an hour.

LADY MACBETH

Yet here's a spot.

DOCTOR

Hark! she speaks! I will set down what comes from her, to satisfy my remembrance the more strongly.

LADY MACBETH

Out, damned spot! out, I say! One, two. Why, then, 'tis time to do't. Hell is murky! Fie, my lord, fie! a soldier, and afeard? What need we fear who knows it, when none can call our power to account? Yet who would have thought the old man to have had so much blood in him.

DOCTOR

Do you mark that?

LADY MACBETH

The Thane of Fife had a wife. Where is she now? What, will these hands ne'er be clean? No more o' that, my lord, no more o' that! You mar all with this starting.

DOCTOR

Go to, go to! you have known what you should not.

GENTLEWOMAN

She has spoke what she should not, I am sure of that. Heaven knows what she has known.

LADY MACBETH

Here's the smell of the blood still. All the perfumes of Arabia will not sweeten this little hand. Oh, oh, oh!

DOCTOR

What a sigh is there! The heart is sorely charged.

GENTLEWOMAN

I would not have such a heart in my bosom for the dignity of the whole body.

DOCTOR

Well, well, well—

GENTLEWOMAN

Pray God it be, Sir.

DOCTOR

This disease is beyond my practice. Yet I have known those which have walked in their sleep who have died holily in their beds.

LADY MACBETH

Wash your hands, put on your nightgown, look not so pale!

I tell you yet again, Banquo's buried. He
cannot come out on 's grave.

DOCTOR

Even so?

LADY MACBETH

To bed, to bed! There's knocking at the gate. Come, come,
come, come, give me your hand! What's done cannot be
undone. To bed, to bed, to bed!

Exit

DOCTOR

Will she go now to bed?

GENTLEWOMAN

Directly.

DOCTOR

Foul whisperings are abroad. Unnatural deeds
Do breed unnatural troubles. Infected minds
To their deaf pillows will discharge their secrets.
More needs she the divine than the physician.
God, God forgive us all! Look after her;
Remove from her the means of all annoyance,
And still keep eyes upon her. So, good night.
My mind she has mated, and amazed my sight.
I think, but dare not speak.

GENTLEWOMAN

Good night, good doctor.

Exeunt

SCENE 2
The country near Dunsinane

ACT 5 SCENE 2
LENNOX AND OTHER SCOTTISH LORDS
ARE LEADING A REBEL SCOTTISH ARMY
TO MEET UP WITH MALCOLM'S
ENGLISH ARMY AT BIRNAM WOOD.
THEY DISCUSS MACBETH AND SAY
THAT HIS SOLDIERS OBEY HIM ONLY
BECAUSE THEY ARE AFRAID OF HIM.

Enter MENTEITH, CAITHNESS, ANGUS, LENNOX, *and Soldiers,*
with drum and flags

MENTEITH

The English power is near, led on by Malcolm,
His uncle Siward and the good Macduff.
Revenges burn in them; for their dear causes
Would to the bleeding and the grim alarm
Excite the mortified man.

5.2

DISK LINK

Guess what Shakespeare's more difficult words and phrases mean in the GLOSSARY GAME.

ANGUS

Near Birnam Wood
Shall we well meet them; that way are they coming.

CAITHNESS

Who knows if Donalbain be with his brother?

LENNOX

For certain, Sir, he is not. I have a file
Of all the gentry. There is Siward's son,
And many unrough youths that even now
Protest their first of manhood.

MENTEITH

What does the tyrant?

CAITHNESS

Great Dunsinane he strongly fortifies.
Some say he's mad; others that lesser hate him
Do call it valiant fury; but, for certain,
He cannot buckle his distempered cause
Within the belt of rule.

ANGUS

Now does he feel
His secret murders sticking on his hands.
Now minutely revolts upbraid his faith-breach.
Those he commands move only in command,
Nothing in love. Now does he feel his title
Hang loose about him, like a giant's robe
Upon a dwarfish thief.

MENTEITH

Who then shall blame
His pestered senses to recoil and start,
When all that is within him does condemn
Itself for being there?

CAITHNESS

Well, march we on,
To give obedience where 'tis truly owed.
Meet we the medicine of the sickly weal;
And with him pour we in our country's purge
Each drop of us.

LENNOX

Or so much as it needs
To dew the sovereign flower and drown the weeds.
Make we our march towards Birnam.

Exeunt, marching

ACT 5 SCENE 3

MACBETH HEARS REPORTS OF THE
ENEMY DRAWING NEARER BUT REFUSES
TO LET THEM WORRY HIM UNTIL THE
WITCHES' PROPHECIES ARE FULFILLED.
HE ASKS THE DOCTOR ABOUT LADY
MACBETH. THE DOCTOR REPLIES THAT
HE CANNOT CURE MENTAL ILLNESS
AND MACBETH DISMISSES MEDICINE
AS USELESS.

SCENE 3

A room in the Castle at Dunsinane

Enter MACBETH, DOCTOR, *and Servants*

MACBETH
Bring me no more reports. Let them fly all!
Till Birnam Wood remove to Dunsinane,
I cannot taint with fear. What's the boy Malcolm?
Was he not born of woman? The spirits that know
All mortal consequences have pronounced me thus:
"Fear not, Macbeth. No man that's born of woman
Shall e'er have power upon thee." Then fly, false thanes,
And mingle with the English epicures.
The mind I sway by and the heart I bear
Shall never sag with doubt nor shake with fear.

Enter a SERVANT

The devil damn thee black, thou cream-faced loon!
Where got'st thou that goose look?
SERVANT
There is ten thousand—
MACBETH
                                        Geese, villain?
SERVANT
                                                            Soldiers, Sir.
MACBETH
Go prick thy face, and over-red thy fear,
Thou lily-livered boy. What soldiers, patch?
Death of thy soul! Those linen cheeks of thine
Are counsellors to fear. What soldiers, whey-face?
SERVANT
The English force, so please you.
MACBETH
Take thy face hence.

Exit SERVANT

                                        Seyton!—I am sick at heart,
When I behold—Seyton, I say!—This push
Will cheer me ever, or disseat me now.
I have lived long enough. My way of life
Is fall'n into the sere, the yellow leaf;

And that which should accompany old age,
As honour, love, obedience, troops of friends,
I must not look to have; but, in their stead,
Curses, not loud but deep, mouth-honour, breath,
Which the poor heart would fain deny, and dare not.
Seyton!

Enter SEYTON

SEYTON
What is your gracious pleasure?
MACBETH
                                                        What news more?
SEYTON
All is confirmed, my lord, which was reported.
MACBETH
I'll fight till from my bones my flesh be hacked.
Give me my armour.
SEYTON
                                        'Tis not needed yet.
MACBETH
I'll put it on.
Send out more horses, skirr the country round;
Hang those that talk of fear. Give me mine armour.
(*To the* DOCTOR) How does your patient, doctor?
DOCTOR
                                                                Not so sick,
            my lord,
As she is troubled with thick-coming fancies,
That keep her from her rest.
MACBETH
                                                Cure her of that.
Canst thou not minister to a mind diseased,
Pluck from the memory a rooted sorrow,
Raze out the written troubles of the brain,
And with some sweet oblivious antidote
Cleanse the stuffed bosom of that perilous stuff
Which weighs upon the heart?
DOCTOR
                                                        Therein the patient
Must minister to himself.
MACBETH
Throw physic to the dogs, I'll none of it.
(*To* SEYTON) Come, put mine armour on. Give me my staff.

Seyton, send out. (*To the* DOCTOR) Doctor,
    the thanes fly from me.
(*To* SEYTON) Come, Sir, despatch.
        (*To the* DOCTOR) If thou couldst, doctor, cast
The water of my land, find her disease,
And purge it to a sound and pristine health,
I would applaud thee to the very echo,
That should applaud again.—(*To* SEYTON) Pull't off, I say.—
(*To the* DOCTOR) What rhubarb, senna, or what
        purgative drug,
Would scour these English hence? Hear'st thou of them?

DOCTOR

Ay, my good lord. Your royal preparation
Makes us hear something.

MACBETH

                (*To* SEYTON) Bring it after me.
I will not be afraid of death and bane,
Till Birnam forest come to Dunsinane.

DOCTOR

(*Aside*) Were I from Dunsinane away and clear,
Profit again should hardly draw me here.

Exeunt

ACT 5 SCENE 4
MALCOLM ORDERS HIS SOLDIERS TO TAKE BRANCHES FROM THE TREES IN BIRNAM WOOD TO CAMOUFLAGE THEIR APPROACH TO MACBETH'S CASTLE. SIWARD ADVISES MACDUFF NOT TO BE TOO HOPEFUL ABOUT THE BATTLE. MALCOLM REPORTS THAT MANY OF MACBETH'S SOLDIERS ARE DESERTING HIM.

SCENE 4

In the country near Birnam Wood

Enter MALCOLM, SIWARD *and* YOUNG SIWARD, MACDUFF, MENTEITH, CAITHNESS, ANGUS, LENNOX, ROSS, *and Soldiers, marching, with drum and flags*

MALCOLM

Cousins, I hope the days are near at hand
That chambers will be safe.

MENTEITH

                                We doubt it nothing.

SIWARD

What wood is this before us?

MENTEITH

                                The wood of Birnam.

MALCOLM

Let every soldier hew him down a bough

And bear't before him. Thereby shall we shadow
The numbers of our host and make discovery
Err in report of us.

SOLDIERS

It shall be done.

SIWARD

We learn no other but the confident tyrant
Keeps still in Dunsinane, and will endure
Our setting down before't.

MALCOLM

'Tis his main hope;
For where there is advantage to be given,
Both more and less have given him the revolt,
And none serve with him but constrainèd things
Whose hearts are absent too.

MACDUFF

Let our just censures
Attend the true event, and put we on
Industrious soldiership.

SIWARD

The time approaches
That will with due decision make us know
What we shall say we have and what we owe.
Thoughts speculative their unsure hopes relate,
But certain issue strokes must arbitrate;
Towards which advance the war.

Exeunt, marching

ACT 5 SCENE 5

MACBETH HAS LOST ALMOST ALL
SENSE OF FEAR. SEYTON BRINGS
NEWS THAT LADY MACBETH IS
DEAD AND MACBETH BROODS ON
THE POINTLESSNESS OF LIFE. A
MESSENGER REPORTS THAT BIRNAM
WOOD IS MOVING AND MACBETH
WAITS FOR THE ATTACK. HE IS READY
TO DIE FIGHTING.

SCENE 5

Inside the Castle at Dunsinane

Enter MACBETH, SEYTON, *and Soldiers, with drum and flags*

MACBETH

Hang out our banners on the outward walls.
The cry is still, "They come!" Our castle's strength
Will laugh a siege to scorn. Here let them lie
Till famine and the ague eat them up.
Were they not forced with those that should be ours,
We might have met them dareful, beard to beard,

DISK LINK
Can you remember all the characters, props, and sound effects in this scene? Test yourself in MAKE A SCENE.

And beat them backward home.
(*A cry of women within*)　　　　What is that noise?
SEYTON
It is the cry of women, my good lord.

Exit

MACBETH
I have almost forgot the taste of fears.
The time has been, my senses would have cooled
To hear a night-shriek, and my fell of hair
Would at a dismal treatise rouse and stir
As life were in't. I have supped full with horrors.
Direness, familiar to my slaughterous thoughts
Cannot once start me.

Re-enter SEYTON

　　　　　　　　　　Wherefore was that cry?
SEYTON
The queen, my lord, is dead.
MACBETH
She should have died hereafter;
There would have been a time for such a word.
Tomorrow, and tomorrow, and tomorrow,
Creeps in this petty pace from day to day
To the last syllable of recorded time,
And all our yesterdays have lighted fools
The way to dusty death. Out, out, brief candle!
Life's but a walking shadow, a poor player
That struts and frets his hour upon the stage
And then is heard no more. It is a tale
Told by an idiot, full of sound and fury,
Signifying nothing.

Enter a MESSENGER

Thou comest to use thy tongue. Thy story quickly.
MESSENGER
Gracious my lord,
I should report that which I say I saw,
But know not how to do it.
MACBETH
　　　　　　　　Well, say, Sir.

5.5

MESSENGER
As I did stand my watch upon the hill,
I looked toward Birnam, and anon, methought,
The wood began to move.

MACBETH
                Liar and slave!

MESSENGER
Let me endure your wrath, if't be not so.
Within this three mile may you see it coming;
I say, a moving grove.

MACBETH
            If thou speak'st false,
Upon the next tree shalt thou hang alive,
Till famine cling thee. If thy speech be sooth,
I care not if thou dost for me as much.
I pull in resolution, and begin
To doubt the equivocation of the fiend
That lies like truth. "Fear not, till Birnam Wood
Do come to Dunsinane," and now a wood
Comes toward Dunsinane. Arm, arm, and out!
If this which he avouches does appear,
There is nor flying hence nor tarrying here.
I 'gin to be aweary of the sun,
And wish the estate o' the world were now undone.
Ring the alarm-bell! Blow, wind! come, wreck!
At least we'll die with harness on our back.

Exeunt

SCENE 6
Outside the Castle at Dunsinane

Drum and flags. Enter MALCOLM, SIWARD, MACDUFF, *and their
Army, with boughs*

MALCOLM
Now near enough. Your leafy screens throw down,
And show like those you are. (*To* SIWARD) You, worthy uncle,
Shall, with my cousin, your right-noble son,
Lead our first battle. Worthy Macduff and we
Shall take upon 's what else remains to do,
According to our order.

SIWARD

Fare you well.
Do we but find the tyrant's power tonight,
Let us be beaten, if we cannot fight.

MACDUFF

Make all our trumpets speak, give them all breath,
Those clamourous harbingers of blood and death.

Exeunt

SCENE 7
Another part of the battlefield

Trumpet calls. Enter MACBETH

MACBETH

They have tied me to a stake. I cannot fly,
But, bear-like, I must fight the course. What's he
That was not born of woman? Such a one
Am I to fear, or none.

Enter YOUNG SIWARD

YOUNG SIWARD

What is thy name?

MACBETH

Thou'lt be afraid to hear it.

YOUNG SIWARD

No; though thou call'st thyself a hotter name
Than any is in hell.

MACBETH

My name's Macbeth.

YOUNG SIWARD

The devil himself could not pronounce a title
More hateful to mine ear.

MACBETH

No, nor more fearful.

YOUNG SIWARD

Thou liest, abhorrèd tyrant; with my sword
I'll prove the lie thou speak'st.

They fight and YOUNG SIWARD *is slain*

101

MACBETH

                        Thou wast born of woman,
But swords I smile at, weapons laugh to scorn,
Brandished by man that's of a woman born.

Exit

Trumpet calls. Enter MACDUFF

MACDUFF

That way the noise is. Tyrant, show thy face!
If thou be'st slain and with no stroke of mine,
My wife and children's ghosts will haunt me still.
I cannot strike at wretched kerns, whose arms
Are hired to bear their staves. Either thou, Macbeth,
Or else my sword with an unbattered edge
I sheathe again undeeded. There thou shouldst be.
By this great clatter, one of greatest note
Seems bruited. (*Aside*) Let me find him, fortune!
And more I beg not.

Exit

Trumpet calls. Enter MALCOLM *and* SIWARD

SIWARD

This way, my lord. The castle's gently rendered:
The tyrant's people on both sides do fight;
The noble thanes do bravely in the war;
The day almost itself professes yours,
And little is to do.

MALCOLM

                   We have met with foes
That strike beside us.

SIWARD

               Enter, Sir, the castle.

Exeunt. Trumpet calls

ACT 5 SCENE 8

MACDUFF CONFRONTS MACBETH AND INFORMS HIM THAT HE WAS BORN BY CAESARIAN SECTION AND THEREFORE COULD BE SAID NOT TO BE "OF WOMAN BORN." MACBETH INITIALLY REFUSES TO FIGHT BUT MACDUFF THREATENS TO DISPLAY HIM TO THE PUBLIC AS A TYRANT. MACBETH DECIDES TO GO DOWN FIGHTING AND MACDUFF KILLS HIM.

SCENE 8

Another part of the battlefield

Enter MACBETH

MACBETH

Why should I play the Roman fool, and die
On mine own sword? Whiles I see lives, the gashes
Do better upon them.

Enter MACDUFF

DISK LINK
There's a quotation on this page that will help you play WHO SAID WHAT?

MACDUFF

                     Turn, hellhound, turn!

MACBETH

Of all men else I have avoided thee.
But get thee back! My soul is too much charged
With blood of thine already.

MACDUFF

                    I have no words;
My voice is in my sword, thou bloodier villain
Than terms can give thee out!

They fight

MACBETH

                        Thou losest labour.
As easy may'st thou the intrenchant air
WIth thy keen sword impress as make me bleed.
Let fall thy blade on vulnerable crests.
I bear a charmèd life, which must not yield,
To one of woman born.

MACDUFF

                  Despair thy charm!
And let the angel whom thou still hast served
Tell thee, Macduff was from his mother's womb
Untimely ripped.

MACBETH

Accursèd be that tongue that tells me so,
For it hath cowed my better part of man!
And be these juggling fiends no more believed,

That palter with us in a double sense,
That keep the word of promise to our ear
And break it to our hope. I'll not fight with thee.

MACDUFF

Then yield thee, coward,
And live to be the show and gaze o' the time!
We'll have thee, as our rarer monsters are,
Painted on a pole, and underwrit,
"Here may you see the tyrant."

MACBETH

                                I will not yield,
To kiss the ground before young Malcolm's feet
And to be baited with the rabble's curse.
Though Birnam Wood be come to Dunsinane,
And thou opposed, being of no woman born,
Yet I will try the last. Before my body
I throw my warlike shield. Lay on, Macduff,
And damned be him that first cries, "Hold, enough!"

Exeunt, fighting. Trumpet calls

DISK LINK

Will Macduff beat the dastardly Macbeth? Answer questions on the play and watch them fight in OFF WITH HIS HEAD!

ACT 5 SCENE 9

VICTORY IS WON. SIWARD IS PROUD THAT HIS SON DIED BRAVELY ON THE BATTLEFIELD. MACDUFF BRINGS MACBETH'S HEAD IN FOR ALL TO SEE. HE HAILS MALCOLM AS KING OF SCOTLAND. MALCOLM PROMOTES HIS NOBLES TO EARLS AND INVITES THEM TO HIS CROWNING CEREMONY AT SCONE.

SCENE 9
In the Castle

Enter, with drum and flags, MALCOLM, SIWARD, ROSS, *the other Thanes, and Soldiers*

MALCOLM

I would the friends we miss were safe arrived.

SIWARD

Some must go off; and yet, by these I see,
So great a day as this is cheaply bought.

MALCOLM

Macduff is missing, and your noble son.

ROSS

Your son, my lord, has paid a soldier's debt.
He only lived but till he was a man,
The which no sooner had his prowess confirmed
In the unshrinking station where he fought,
But like a man he died.

SIWARD

                           Then he is dead?

ROSS

    Ay, and brought off the field. Your cause of sorrow
    Must not be measured by his worth, for then
    It hath no end.

SIWARD

                   Had he his hurts before?

ROSS

    Ay, on the front.

SIWARD

                   Why then, God's soldier be he!
    Had I as many sons as I have hairs,
    I would not wish them to a fairer death.
    And so, his knell is knolled.

MALCOLM

                   He's worth more sorrow,
    And that I'll spend for him.

SIWARD

                   He's worth no more.
    They say he parted well, and paid his score,
    And so, God be with him! Here comes newer comfort.

Enter MACDUFF, *with* MACBETH'S *head*

MACDUFF

    Hail, King! for so thou art. Behold, where stands
    The usurper's cursèd head. The time is free.
    I see thee compassed with thy kingdom's pearl,
    That speak my salutation in their minds;
    Whose voices I desire aloud with mine:
    Hail, King of Scotland!

ALL

                   Hail, King of Scotland!

Fanfare

MALCOLM

    We shall not spend a large expense of time
    Before we reckon with your several loves,
    And make us even with you. My thanes and kinsmen,
    Henceforth be earls, the first that ever Scotland
    In such an honour named. What's more to do,
    Which would be planted newly with the time,
    As calling home our exiled friends abroad
    That fled the snares of watchful tyranny;

Producing forth the cruel ministers
Of this dead butcher and his fiend-like queen,
Who, as 'tis thought, by self and violent hands
Took off her life—this, and what needful else
That calls upon us, by the grace of Grace,
We will perform in measure, time and place.
So, thanks to all at once and to each one,
Whom we invite to see us crowned at Scone.

Fanfare. Exeunt

Running Your Interfact Shakespeare Disk

Your INTERFACT SHAKESPEARE CD-ROM will run both on PCs with Windows and on Apple Macintosh computers.

To make sure that your computer meets the system requirements, check the list below.

Minimum System Requirements

PC
- Pentium 166Mhz or faster processor
- Windows 95+PC
- 32Mb RAM
- 16-bit color display
- Soundcard
- 640 x 480 graphics

Apple Macintosh
- PowerMacs and above (200Mhz processor)
- System 8.1 (or later)
- 32Mb RAM
- Color monitor set to at least 640 x 480 graphics
- 16-bit color display

LOADING YOUR INTERFACT SHAKESPEARE DISK

INTERFACT SHAKESPEARE is easy to use. You can run INTERFACT SHAKESPEARE from the CD-ROM, so all you have to do is place it in the appropriate drive of your computer—you do not need to install the program on your hard drive. Before you begin, quickly run through the checklist below to ensure that your computer is ready to run INTERFACT SHAKESPEARE.

PC WITH WINDOWS

The program should start automatically when you put the disk in the CD-ROM drive. If it does not, follow these instructions:
1 Put the disk in the CD-ROM drive of your computer
2 Double-click MY COMPUTER
3 Double-click CD-ROM drive icon
4 Double-click on the MACBETH icon to start

APPLE MACINTOSH

1 Put the disk in the CD-ROM drive of your computer
2 Double-click on the INTERFACT SHAKESPEARE icon
3 Double-click on the MACBETH icon to start

CHECKLIST

◆ First, make sure that your computer and monitor meet the system requirements on page 107.

◆ Make sure that your computer, monitor, and CD-ROM drive are all switched on and working properly.

◆ It is important that you don't have other applications running, such as word processors. Before starting INTERFACT SHAKESPEARE, quit all other applications.

◆ Make sure any screen savers for your computer have been switched off.

How to Use Interfact Shakespeare

INTERFACT SHAKESPEARE is easy to use. First find out how to load the program (see page 108) then read these simple instructions and dive in!

There are seven different features to explore. Use the shield buttons at the bottom of the screen to select a feature or a game. You will see that the main area of the screen changes when you click on different features.

For example, this is what your screen will look like when you play MAKE A SCENE, a game where you try to remember some of the characters, props, and sound effects in certain scenes of the play. Each game comes with instructions and help text.

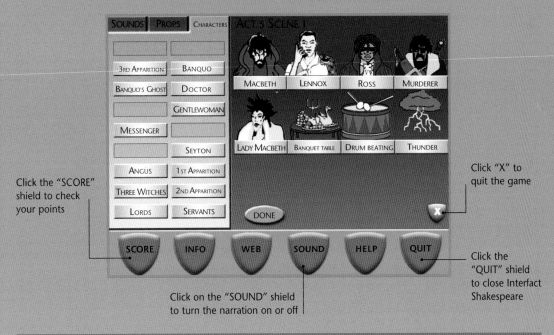

Click the "SCORE" shield to check your points

Click "X" to quit the game

Click the "QUIT" shield to close Interfact Shakespeare

Click on the "SOUND" shield to turn the narration on or off

DISK LINKS

When you read the play, you'll come across Disk Links. These show you where to find activities on the CD-ROM that relate to the page that you are reading. Watch for Disk Links as they will help you score more points when you play the games on the disk!

BOOKMARKS

As you use the games and features on the disk, you'll see Bookmarks. These give you page references in the book which will help you to play the games. Just turn to the page of the book shown in the Bookmark and you'll find the answer you need.

INFORMATION

For easy-to-access information about the play, click on the "INFO" shield on the main menu of the disk. The Time Line and Meet the Characters screens give an overview of who's who and the play's main events. For further information, click on the Web link.

DISK LINK
Can you remember all the characters, props, and sound effects in this scene? Test yourself in MAKE A SCENE.

and his son, Fleance, must be killed. He employs some murderers to carry out the assassination.

Page 54

Characters

Time Line

GAMES   SCORE   INFO   WEB

HOT DISK TIPS

◆ If you need help finding your way around the CD-ROM, click on the "HELP" shield to go to the help section. This gives you information on how to access each feature, how to play the games, and scoring.

◆ Click on the main screen to move on at any time. Use the "QUIT" button to exit the CD-ROM and use the "X" button to close the game you are in, or to close a popup.

◆ Keep a close eye on the cursor. When it changes from an arrow to a hand, click your mouse and something will happen.

TROUBLESHOOTING

If you have a problem with your INTERFACT SHAKESPEARE CD-ROM, you should find the solution here. If you can't, first try contacting us for assistance by e-mail: helpline@two-canpublishing.com. If you do not get a response, call the telephone helpline on 609 921 6700. Leave a message and we will get back to you as soon as we can.

> **Run through these general checkpoints before consulting Common Problems on the next page.**

YOUR COMPUTER SETUP

Resetting the screen resolution in Windows 95 or 98:

Click on START at the bottom left of your screen, then click on SETTINGS, then CONTROL PANEL, then double-click on DISPLAY. Click on the SETTINGS tab at the top.

Reset the Desktop area (or Display area) to 640 x 480 pixels and choose 16-bit color display, then click APPLY.

You may need to restart your computer after changing the display settings.

Adjusting the Virtual Memory in Windows 95 or 98:

It is not recommended that these settings are adjusted because Windows will automatically configure your system as required.

Adjusting the Virtual Memory on Apple Macintosh:

If you have 32Mb of RAM or more, MACBETH will run faster. If you do not have this amount of RAM free, hard disk memory can be used by switching on Virtual Memory. Select the APPLE MENU, CONTROL PANELS, then MEMORY. Switch on VIRTUAL MEMORY. Set the amount of memory you require, then restart.

CD-ROM will not run

There may not be enough memory available. Quit all other applications. If this does not work, increase your machine's RAM by adjusting the Virtual Memory (see page 111).

There is no sound
(Try each of the following)

1 Make sure that your speakers or headphones are connected to the speaker outlet at the back of your computer. Make sure they are not plugged into the audio socket next to the CD-ROM drive at the front of the computer.
2 Make sure the volume control is turned up (on your external speakers and by using internal volume control).
3 (PCs only) Your soundcard is not SoundBlaster compatible. To make your settings SoundBlaster compatible, see your soundcard manual for more information.

Graphics are missing or poor quality

Not enough memory is available or you have the wrong display setting. Either quit other applications and programs or make sure that your monitor control is set to 16-bit color display.

Graphics freeze or text boxes appear blank (Windows 95 or 98)

Graphics card acceleration is too high. Right-click your mouse on MY COMPUTER. Click on PROPERTIES, then PERFORMANCE, then GRAPHICS. Reset the hardware acceleration slider to "None." Click OK. Restart your computer.

Your machine freezes

There is not enough memory available. Either quit other applications and programs or increase your machine's RAM by adjusting the Virtual Memory (see page 111).